# Decolonizing African Religions

*A Short History of African Religions
in Western Scholarship*

# DECOLONIZING AFRICAN RELIGIONS

*A Short History of African Religions in Western Scholarship*

---

Okot p'Bitek

*Introduction by*
Kwasi Wiredu

DIASPORIC AFRICA PRESS
New York

This book is a publication of

DIASPORIC AFRICA PRESS
NEW YORK | WWW.DAFRICAPRESS.COM

*African Religion in Western Scholarship* by Okot P'Bitek. Copyright © The Estate of Okot P'Bitek. Reprinted by permission of estate manager, Jane Bitek Langoya.
Introduction © by Kwasi Wiredu. Reprinted by permission of the author and the *African Studies Quarterly*.

New revised edition, copyright © 2011 by Diasporic Africa Press

All rights reserved. No part of this publication may be reproduced, stored in a retrieval system, or transmitted, in any form or by any means, electronic, mechanical, photocopying, recording, or otherwise, without the prior permission of the author.

Library of Congress Control Number: 2011921108

Okot P'Bitek, *Decolonizing African Religion: A Short History of African Religions in Western Scholarship.* Introduction by Kwasi Wiredu.
Includes bibliographical references and index.

ISBN 978-0-966-02015-1 (pbk. : alk. paper)

*Special discounts are available for bulk purchases of this book. For more information, please contact us at sales@dafricapress.com.*

Diasporic Africa Press uses environmentally friendly book materials, including recycled text paper that is composed of at least 30 percent post-consumer waste, whenever possible.

Printed in the United States of America on acid-free paper

# Contents

Preface     vii

Introduction: Decolonizing African Philosophy and Religion     xi
   *Kwasi Wiredu*

I. Social Anthropology and Colonialism     1

II. What is Tribe?     5

III. The Classical European World and Africa     9

IV. Superstitions of Western Man     15

V. Studies in African Religions, ca. 1970     19

VI. Dialogue with Animism     25

VII. Max Muller, The Missionaries and African Deities     29

VIII. What then is Jok?     35

IX. Hellenization of African Deities     39

X. De-Hellenizing the Christian God     43

XI. Some Conclusions     49

   Selected Bibliography     57

   Notes     61

   Index     69

# Preface

*I am Ignorant of the Good Word in the Clean Book*[1]

My husband [Ocol]
Looks down upon me;
He says
I am a mere pagan,
I do not know
The way of God.
He says I am ignorant
Of the good word
In the Clean Book
And I do not have A Christian name.

Ocol dislikes me
Because, he says,
*Jok* is in my head
And I like visiting
The diviner-priest
Like my mother!
He says
He is ashamed of me
Because when the *jok*
In my head
Has been provoked
It throws me down
As if I have fits.

Ocol laughs at me
Because I cannot
Cross myself properly
    *In the name of the Father*
    *And of the Son And the Clean Ghost*

And I do not understand
The confession,
And I fear
The bushy-faced, fat-bellied padre
Before whom people kneel
When they pray.

I refused to join
The Protestant catechist class
Because I did not want
To become a house-girl,
[…] Oh how young girls
Labor to buy a name!
You break your back
Drawing water
For the wives
Of the teachers

The skin of your hand
Hardens and peels off
Grinding millet and *simsim*.
You hoe their fields,
Split firewood,
You cut grass for thatching
And for starting fires,
You smear their floors
With cow dung and black soil
And harvest their crops.

And when they are eating
They send you to play games
To play the board game
Under the mango tree!
And girls gather
Wild sweet potatoes
And eat them raw
As if there is a famine

[…] You work as if
You are a newly eloped girl!
The wives of protestant
Church teachers and priests
Are a happy lot.
They sit with their legs stretched out
And bask in the morning sun,
All they know
Is hatching a lot of children.

My elder sister
Was christened Erina,
She was a Protestant
But she suffered bitterly

In order to buy the name.
And her loin beads
No longer fitted her!

One Sunday
I followed her
Into the Protestant church:
A big man stood
Before the people.
His hand was lifted up,
My sister said
He was blessing the people.

The man had no rosary,
He wore a long black gown
And a wide white robe
He held a little shiny saucer:
It had small pieces of something.
The name of the man
Was Eliya
And he was calling people
To come and eat
Human flesh!
He put little bits
In their hands
And they ate it up!

Then he took a cup,
Pie said
There was human blood
In the cup
And he gave it
To the people
To drink!
I ran out of the church, I was very sick!
O! Protestants eat people!
They are all wizards,
They exhume corpses for dinner!

I once joined
The Catholic Evening Speakers' Class

But I did not stay long
I ran away,
I ran away from shouting

Meaninglessly in the evenings
Like parrots
Like the crow birds
>Maria the Clean Woman
>Mother of the Hunchback
>Pray for us
>Who spoil things
>Full of graciya.

The things they shout
I do not understand,
They shout anyhow
They shout like mad people.
The padre shouts words,
You cannot understand,
And he does not seem
To care in the least
Whether his hearers
Understand him or not;
A strange language they speak
These Christian diviner-priests,
And the white nuns
Think the girls understand
What they are saying
And are annoyed
When the girls laugh....

The above lines come from Ugandan writer and scholar Okot p'Bitek (1931–82) in his most famous poem, *Song of Lawino*, which satirically dealt with issues rooted in the conflicts between (Western) European and African cultures. In the discourse of the imposition of European ideals, Africa's voice is found in the mouth of rural dweller Lawino, whereas Europe's lies in the person of Ocol, her European-schooled husband. No doubt due to the publication and wide popularly enjoyed by the *Song of Lawino*, p'Bitek became one of the most original poets and social critics of twentieth-century Africa.

Okot p'Bitek was born in the northern Ugandan town of Gulu in 1931 and he began writing at an early age. Though he is best known for *Song of Lawino* (translated from the original Luo, *Wer pa Lawino*), p'Bitek was also an able scholar, having earned a law degree from University of Wales at Aberystwyth and a degree in social anthropology at Oxford University. His most notable yet least recognized piece of scholarship came in the form of his *African Religions in Western Scholarship*. We are reprinting this work, along with a new introduction by Ghanaian philosopher Kwasi Wiredu, in hopes of reintroducing this classic work to a new generation, especially for those with an interest in African spiritual cultures or "religions" and in need of "decolonizing" them so that they be studied, appreciated, and engaged on their own cultural and historic terms.

# Introduction
## Decolonizing African Philosophy and Religion

Kwasi Wiredu

**Particularistic Studies of African Philosophies as an Aid to Decolonization**

Let me begin by defining what I mean by decolonization in African philosophy. By decolonization, I mean divesting African philosophical thinking of all undue influences emanating from our colonial past. The crucial word in this formulation is "undue." Obviously, it would not be rational to try to reject everything of a colonial ancestry. Conceivably, a thought or a mode of inquiry spearheaded by our erstwhile colonizers may be valid or in some way beneficial to humankind. Are we called upon to reject or ignore it? That would be a madness having neither rhyme nor reason.

Yet there are reasons for adopting a doubly critical stance toward the problems and theories of Western philosophy—particularly toward the categories of thought embedded therein. The reasons are historical. Colonialism was not only a political imposition, but also a cultural one. Gravely affected, or even perhaps infected, were our religions and systems of education. I will address the question of religion later, but I want directly to notice an aspect of the system of education introduced by colonialism that is of a particular philosophical relevance. It consists in the fact that education was delivered in the medium of one foreign language or another.

Now if you learn philosophy in a given language, that is the language in which you naturally philosophize, not just during the learning period but also, all things being equal, for life. But a language, most assuredly, is not conceptually neutral; syntax and vocabulary are apt to suggest definite modes of conceptualization. Note, however, that I say "suggest," not "compel," for, if the phenomenon had the element of necessitation implied by the latter word, no decolonization would be possible. Nevertheless, the starting point of the problem is that the African who has learned philosophy in English, for example, has most likely become conceptually westernized to a large extent not by choice but by the force of historical circumstances. To that same extent he may have become de-Africanized. It does not matter if the philosophy learned was African philosophy. If that philosophy was academically formulated in English and articulated therein, the message was already substantially westernized, unless there was a conscious effort toward cross-cultural filtration. Of course, in colonial times such concerns were not the order of the day, to say the least, nor have they, even now in post-colonial times, acquired that status....

It will have been gathered already that philosophical decolonization is necessarily a conceptual enterprise; it is not just a critique of doctrine but also of fundamental conceptualization. I use "critique" here in the sense of an examination of validity rather than the exposure of invalidity. Indeed, philosophy, or at any rate the best kind of philosophy, is a critique, for the most part, of fundamental conceptualization. That is to say, it is the critical examination of the conceptual framework upon which the thought of a culture is erected. English philosophers, for example, brought up on the Western tradition of thought, are not supposed to take Western categories for granted. That would be to wallow in the unexamined life. They are expected to examine their conceptual inheritance afresh, as far as practicable, and this must be done on two fronts. First, they must review the accumulation of technical vocabularies presented in the tradition together, of course, with the associated theories. These often depart, sometimes quite radically, from common modes of conceptualization, although they may have some basic links with them. A technical heritage can have quite a commanding influence in the life of a culture. Yet, there is nothing sacrosanct about it, and philosophical genius sometimes consists in subverting good portions of it.

There is also a common-language front, for technical vocabulary is a specialization of common language and may owe some of its characteristics to that origin. It is this link that gives technical philosophy much of its cultural identity. Consider, for example, the use of the word "idea" in British empiricism. By "idea" Locke says he means the immediate object of our perception. But it turns out that he takes this to mean a sensation. Since a sensation is a condition of the human body, this means that the table I perceive is a state of myself, if it is an idea. Locke wavered on this, but Berkeley and Hume asserted it without any inhibition. Indeed, by the time we reach Hume, the perceived table has become a momentary state, not a perduring object, and the perceiver too has become nothing but the same momentary state without a possessor. This concept of a perceived object would puzzle any ordinary native speaker innocent of empiricist sophistication into fits. Yet, on the other hand, the straightforwardly substantive status of the word "idea" in English and its objectual idioms seem to facilitate making it into an object in an ontologically serious sense, at least to start with. The point now is that an analogue of this does not occur in every language. Obviously, in languages of a contrary tendency it would take an uncommon taste for paradox for one to come up with the empiricist idea. This suggests that in examining conceptual formations at the level of the technical discourse, philosophers need also to keep a critical eye on the conceptual intimations of the natural languages in which they work.

The situation is more complex in the case of Africans who have been trained in some foreign philosophical tradition—for instance, English-speaking philosophy—for there is now a cross-cultural dimension. They must assume both of the critical duties just noticed. But in addition, they must not forget that they have their own languages which have their own conceptual suggestiveness calling for critical study; which is why I said early on that African philosophers have to be doubly critical. Clearly, African philosophy at this historical juncture has, of necessity, to be comparative. This comparative approach is required not only when African philosophers work in areas of discourse called African philosophy in so many words but also in all philosophical work on all philosophical topics whatsoever. In particular, African philosophers should not wait until they are doing courses specifically designated African philosophy before they bring their African conceptual resources to bear on their treatments of issues. Whether it be in logic, or epistemology, or ethics, or metaphysics, or whatever, they must introduce African inputs wherever feasible.

I think that it is a colonial type of mentality that regards African philosophy as something that should be kept apart from the mainstream of philosophical thinking. Compare how things stand or might stand in, say, the study of British philosophy. Surely, it would be more than mildly idiosyncratic for a British teacher of philosophy in a British university to propose, in his teaching of metaphysics, for example, to hold in abeyance all metaphysical insights deriving from British sources until s/he has the occasion to teach a course on British philosophy. In fact, there may be no such course in the given British university for the good reason that there may be no need for it. It would be a great day for African philosophy when the same becomes true of an African university, for it would mean that African insights have become fully integrated into the principal branches of philosophy.

That time has not come yet. In colonial times little, if anything, was heard about African philosophy. I finished my undergraduate studies in philosophy in Ghana in 1958 just a year after our independence from Britain. In the whole of that period of philosophical study not a single word was said about African philosophy, nor, indeed, was the phrase "African philosophy" ever mentioned. In all fairness, my teachers cannot be blamed for this. They were hired to teach us Western philosophy, and that is what they did. Actually, it probably would have been an advantage if contemporary African philosophers had had to begin with a totally clean slate when they began in post-independence times to research into African philosophy. But, as it happens, religious and anthropological studies had been made of African worldviews in departments of religion and anthropology, and these tended to contain elements relevant to African philosophy. Now, although these studies were not technically philosophical, they were conducted not only in foreign languages, such as English, French and German, but also in terms of categories of Western metaphysical thought that have become widely received in Western culture. To take only a few examples, consider such categories of thought as those contained in the following dichotomies: the spiritual versus the physical, the supernatural versus the natural, the mystical versus the non-mystical, the religious versus the secular, being versus nothingness. These are modes of conceptualization that are very deeply entrenched in Western thought. I do not mean to suggest that every Western thinker believes that there are things falling under one side or the other of each of these dichotomies. What I think is the case is that most Western thinkers would find these dichotomies at least intelligible. Thus even a Western religious skeptic, while denying that there are any spiritual or supernatural beings, may, nevertheless, at the same time grant that the notion of a spiritual entity is not meaningless. Only logical positivists, and perhaps a few others, have wanted to say that such notions are meaningless. But the requiem for logical positivism is generally considered to be concluded.

When African thought was approached with intellectual categories such as the ones just mentioned some quite lopsided results ensued, although they did not seem to bother people much. Some of the findings of this sort of study of African thought that were, and still are, assiduously disseminated are that Africans see the world as being full of spiritual entities, that Africans are religious in all things, not even separating the secular from the religious, that African thought is, through and through, mystical, and so on. Some African philosophers have followed this way of talking of African thought quite cheerfully. One reason may be that in their academic training they may themselves have come to internalize such accounts of African thought so thoroughly that they have become part of the furniture of their minds. Such minds are what may justly be called colonized. They are minds that think about and expound their own culture in terms of categories of a colonial origin without any qualms as to any possible conceptual incongruities. Such a mode of thinking may correctly be said to be unduly influenced by the historical accident of colonization. It may well be that if the concepts in question had been critically examined, they might have been found to be appropriate, but it may very well also be that they might have been found to be inapplicable in the context of African thought. In either case, an important preliminary question would have been answered and the way cleared for potentially enlightening accounts of African thought and its continuation in the modern world. In either case, moreover, the old accounts would have been decolonized.

In the negative case, that is, in the case in which critical inquiry discovers a foreign category of thought to be inapplicable within African thinking, an additional question of the greatest philosophical interest arises. If those categories do not make sense in African thought, does the fault lie in the concepts themselves or in African thought? I suspect that sometimes it will be the one and other times, the other. But we won't find out if we don't investigate, and if we don't investigate, then we wallow in colonized thinking. What makes the difference, then, between decolonized and colonized thinking is what I am in the habit of calling due reflection in our approach to discourses about African thought framed in foreign categories.

I have so far been talking of categories of thought, that is, fundamental concepts by means of which whole ranges of issues are formulated and discussed. But the question of decolonization also affects particular propositions expressed in terms of those categories. As an intellectual package, Christianity, for example, consists of particular metaphysical and ethical propositions. Any African who espouses Christianity without critical examination at some point of the truth or falsity of its propositions, or the validity of their supporting arguments, where there are any, must incur the label of being an intellectually colonized African. (I say "at some point" because many of us are already Christians by the time we have emerged from elementary school without ever having had the occasion to pose the question.)

On the other hand, if one goes along with the Christian package after due reflection, then one is entitled to be exempted from the colonized description. This point is worth emphasizing. An African is not to be debited with the colonial mentality merely because s/he espouses Christianity or Islam or any other foreign religion. It just may be that salvation lies elsewhere than in African religions. But an African should not take it for granted that this is the case simply from having been brought up in a foreign religion. The issue, in other words, needs to be confronted in the spirit of due reflection.

One way in which some Africans have seemed to want to evade this intellectual responsibility has been to say that religion is a matter of faith rather than reason and that, therefore, any critical probing is out of place. This expedient can be viewed from more than one unflattering perspective, but the following consideration should expose adequately the logical futility of the maneuver. Where two religions are in question, in this case, the indigenous African religion and Christianity, the suggestion that religion is a matter of faith is clearly incapable of explaining a preference of one over the other. Moreover, ordinary common sense dictates that one should not jettison what is one's own, in favor of what has come from abroad, for no reason at all. It is, accordingly, difficult to see the faith defense as anything other than the rationalization of an intellectual inertia born of an early subjection to evangelism, that is to say, a colonized condition of the mind.

It is, as noted above, possible for Africans to be Christians in a non-colonized manner, but it is not clear that such Africans are always eager to acknowledge the widespread consequences of that persuasion for the evaluation of African religions. There are, as I will suggest later, definite incompatibilities between Christianity and various African religions. These are not incompatibilities that lie at the peripheries of these religions; they go to the roots. Consequently, an African who espouses Christianity on due reflection may have to admit frankly, and with stated reasons, that s/he rejects the religion indigenous to his or her culture. There is nothing wrong with this in principle. What is wrong is the apparent attempt on the part of some African Christians to have it both ways.

It is probably clear without further argument that the exorcising of the colonial mentality in African philosophy is going to involve conceptually critical studies of African traditional philosophies. I might mention that African philosophy consists of both a traditional and a modern component. It would have been unnecessary to make a point that, in the abstract, sounds so trite, were it not for the fact that some people seem to equate African philosophy with traditional African philosophy. It is, in any case, perhaps not so trite to insist that the imperative of decolonization applies to both phases of African philosophy.

As far as contemporary African philosophizing is concerned, it is important to understand that the imperative of decolonization does not enjoin anything like parochialism. There are cardinal branches of philosophical learning that were not developed in African traditions in most parts of Africa south of the Sahara. These include the disciplines of logic and its philosophy and the philosophy of mathematics and natural science. I have called for the domestication, in Africa, of disciplines such as these in previous writings, and I would like to take this opportunity to make a clarification. By domestication I do not mean the mindless copying of conclusions arrived at somewhere else. I mean taking up broad intellectual concerns relating to certain subject matters.

Consider logic. In our traditional life we do argue and we do evaluate arguments both with respect to their validity and soundness. In their disputations our elders are even wont to enunciate fundamental logical principles such as the laws of non-contradiction (viz. nothing is both the case and not the case) and excluded middle (viz. something is either the case or not the case). For example, among the Akans of Ghana, inconsistent talk before any group of elders would be likely to invite the reminder that *nokware mu nni abra*, literally, there is no conflict in truth, which, evidently, is an invocation of the principle of non-contradiction. And trying to evade an option as well as its contradictory will earn you the censure *kosi a enkosi, koda a enkoda*, that is, you will not stand and you will not lie! The latter form of remonstrance, which is a stern way of trying to wake somebody up to the principle of excluded middle, is, in fact, so common that the logical carelessness in question will trigger it among almost any group of Akans, not just the elders.

Nevertheless, we do not, to my knowledge, have in Ghana the tradition of logical study as a formal discipline. It does not appear that we have formed within our traditions the habit of trying to set out the principles of reasoning, among which non-contradiction and excluded middle are of a very basic importance, in the manner of a system (as in logic). Nor, consequently, have we tended to investigate the assortment of theoretical questions that arise in such an enterprise (as in the philosophy of logic). For Africans to apply their minds to these projects, taking advantage of whatever insights may currently be available internationally in these areas of investigation, is for them to try to domesticate the disciplines concerned, in this case logic and the philosophy of logic. Since in the modern world Western logicians and philosophers have been engaged in these kinds of researches for a considerable time, there is no doubt but that the African who looks at their results might find something useful to build on. In this sort of thing, to be sure, there would be no wisdom in trying to reinvent the wheel.

Even so, in any such pursuits Africans will have to be doubly critical in the manner already explained. To attend to logic a little further: This discipline is a certain kind of study in syntax and semantics. Although it is fashionable to call the systems that are constructed and studied therein artificial languages, it cannot be supposed that these "languages" are totally independent of the natural languages in which the constructions are initiated. It is not inconceivable, therefore, that some aspects of the results obtained, especially in the philosophical reaches of the researches, may depend on characteristics of the syntax and semantics of the particular natural languages involved that are neither universal nor necessary to all natural languages. Africans working in these areas will have to be especially alert to this possibility lest they multiply concepts and concerns beyond necessity. Still, it is eminently reasonable to expect that there are some things of a universal validity in these disciplines, cross-culturally speaking. For example, if the simplest form of conditionality required for defining the relation between the premises and the conclusion of a valid argument must involve the notion of necessity, this will be so in Europe and America as well as in Africa, China, Japan, etc. Whatever the truth in regard to this question, it is of no consequence where its discoverer comes from. This is the basis of the possibility both that we in Africa can learn something from the West and that the West, too, can learn something from us.

Decolonization, then, has nothing to do with the attitude which implies that Africans should steer clear of those philosophical disciplines that have at this particular point in human history received their greatest development in the West. Africans who take this view cannot, in any case, hold it consistently across all academic disciplines. They will have to have a strange mentality indeed to advocate, for example, stopping the study of mathematics and natural science in African universities. But if these disciplines are admitted, then why stop short of their philosophies? If Africans do not enter these areas of philosophy and make their presence felt in them, they will in perpetuity remain outsiders to the project of understanding and clarifying modes of thought that have played a huge part in the making of the modern world. Worse, they will have to call, at least occasionally, upon the help of those peoples who have mastered the relevant specialities; this means that they will be in a state of perpetual dependence.

Without prejudice to the foregoing reflections, however, it is clear that, for historical reasons, this is the time for the greatest decolonizing attention to be paid to the study of traditional African philosophy. Since, as already noted, decolonization is a highly conceptual process, this implies that there will have to be intensive studies of those elements of culture that play significant roles in the constitution of meanings in the various African worldviews. Of these, language stands preeminent. One cannot hope to disentangle the conceptual impositions that have historically been made upon African thought-formations without a close understanding of the indigenous languages concerned. This immediately prescribes a certain methodology in the study of African traditional philosophy. Put simply, it stipulates that emphasis should be given to detailed, in-depth studies of the traditional philosophies of specific African peoples by researchers who know the languages involved well. (This, I might emphasize, is a policy of emphasis not of exclusion. Other types of work, such as those of the domesticating type alluded to above, will also have to go on.)

Sometimes there are pressures on African philosophers to venture continent-wide generalizations about African philosophy. Perhaps, sometimes, available information permits judicious generalizations of this scope. For example, a communalist outlook seems to be quite widespread in traditional life on the continent. This would lead one to expect a certain type of ethical orientation, but any such inferences, even if they seem to be supported by the anthropological data, will still need to be substantiated by linguistically informed and conceptually critical philosophical studies of the particular people concerned.

Such studies are what I call *particularistic* studies. They take the form of inquiries into topics such as "The Yoruba Conception of a Person," "The Chewa Notion of the Afterlife," "The Akan Conception of God," "The Nuer Notion of Spirit," "The Zulu Conception of Morality," and so on. Notice the concepts involved in these titles: Person, Afterlife, God, Spirit, Morality. Do these concepts have unproblematic counterparts in the language and thought of the people concerned? In any case, how do the African concepts that one has in mind compare and contrast with these concepts as they occur in Western thought or, more strictly, in various brands of Western thought? (This verbal circumspection is necessary owing to the fact that Western thought is not a monolithic structure but rather a variegated one, rich in diverse modes of conceptualization.)

The questions just raised are preliminary issues needing to be settled before we can take up issues of validity or truth. Clearly, they are issues whose treatment will require extensive knowledge of the relevant languages. That knowledge will have to be brought to bear upon the evaluation of specific philosophical attributions to various African peoples couched in terms of concepts such as the ones noted above. At present, particularistic studies in the literature have too precipitously tended to take cross-cultural equivalences for granted with regard to the concepts mentioned and a large range of others. This has meant that wittingly or most likely unwittingly, African conceptions of the relevant subjects have been assimilated to Western ones. It is a remarkable fact that this conceptual superimposition can occur even in the process of an attempt to point out differences.

Consider the following example. Father Tempels in his *Bantu Philosophy* explains that the Western conception of being is static while the African counterpart is dynamic. The latter is, he says, dynamic in the following sense. For Africans, "Being is force and force is being." In the face of a message of this sort, formulated in a foreign language, I recommend that African philosophers should ask themselves the following question, which, on the face of it, but perhaps only on the face of it, is quite a simple question. How is the thesis proffered to be expressed in my vernacular? This is a question that our training in foreign languages tends to make us forget to ask. By contrast, many other peoples think philosophically in their own vernaculars as a matter of course.

In this matter I have tried to do as I preach with the following result: Zero! The thing cannot be done. The thesis cannot be expressed in my language, namely, the Akan language spoken in Ghana and the Ivory Coast. In this language, unlike, say, English, there is no such thing as the existential verb "to be." The only possible renditions of the notion of "being" are either predicative or adverbial. To be or being always prompts the question, "To be what, where?" or, "Being what, where?" The Akan expression for "to be" is *wo ho* or *ye*. The word *wo* in this context is syncategorematic; it is incomplete, requiring some specification of place, however indeterminate. Thus *wo ho* means "is there, at some place." Similarly, *ye* cannot stand alone; it needs a complement, such as in *ye onipa* (is a person) or *ye tenten* (is long). Thus the best that one can do in rendering the existential use of "being" would be to say something like, "*Se biribi wo ho*," which translates back to English as "The circumstance that something is there, at some place." Good sense forbids trying to go any further in the experiment of casting, "Being is force and force is being," in Akan.

The conclusion to which this ill-fated thought experiment brings us is that the thesis in question cannot rightly be attributed to the Akans. Apart from the intrinsic interest of this finding, it is of some relevance to the evaluation of Tempels's account as he often writes as if he thought that what is true of the Bantu is true of all Africans. We, on our part, however, do recognize that if it cannot be attributed to the Akans, it does not follow that it cannot be attributed to the Bantus that Tempels studied. Decolonization in African philosophy does not imply forcing philosophical unanimity upon the diverse peoples of Africa. As it happens, however, the late Alexis Kagame, a Bantu philosopher and scientific linguist, also argued that the existential verb "to be" does not occur in the Bantu group of languages, and pointed out that the Bantu analogue of "to be" always prompts the question, "To be what, where?" If Kagame is right, then whatever it was that Tempels noticed about Bantu thought was radically misstated by the use of an inapplicable Western category of thought, namely, the concept of being as existentially construed. It is a concept that was obviously deeply ingrained in Tempels's own manner of thinking, and he very well may have thought it universal to all human thinking. Since some concepts are actually universal, no necessary opprobrium should attach to Tempels's apparent procedure. Nevertheless, the necessity for a critical examination of accounts of African thought such as Tempels's, with an eye to the unraveling of any conceptual superimpositions, remains undiminished. And it is fair to say that Africans who go about disseminating Tempels's claim without confronting the conceptual issue are simply advertising their colonial mentality for all who have eyes to see.

Let us be clear about one thing. That the existential notion of being cannot be rendered in Akan or, if Kagame is right, in the Bantu group of languages, does not in itself show that there is anything wrong with it. As previously suggested, it may possibly be that these African languages are inadequate and are in need of a supplementation in this regard. On the other hand, it may be that this existential concept of being is a semantically defective concept, notwithstanding its great currency in Western metaphysics. This is a separate question. All that our remarks show, if they are right, is that the view that, "Being is force and force is being," cannot be attributed to the Akans or the Bantus for a deep semantic reason. Should it enter the head of an Akan or Bantu metaphysician to argue that the Akan or Bantu way of expressing the notion ostensibly expressed in English by the existential verb "to be" is metaphysically superior to the Western construal as evidenced in Tempels's sentence and in certain even more famous sentences in Western metaphysics, that contention will have to be argued on what I have called independent grounds. I mean by that, considerations that are independent of the peculiarities of the given vernaculars and are, therefore, intelligible to all concerned irrespective of language, race, persuasion, etc. The possibility of independent considerations, by the way, is a precondition of inter-cultural dialogue. And the possibility of this last, we might note parenthetically, is the refutation of relativism.

Another thing we ought to be clear about in this connection is that the linguistic considerations involved in any African philosopher's attempts at conceptual decolonization need not be above debate. On the contrary, any such debate is a sign of a decolonizing vitality; for, remember, the hallmark of decolonized thinking is due reflection not durable deference among African thinkers.

There are still other things to be noted. The very idea of a communal philosophy that is entailed in the notion of particularistic studies of traditional African philosophies might be put in question. It might be suggested that to talk of the Bantu conception of this or the Zulu conception of that is to postulate a unanimity or consensus in philosophical belief among the traditional peoples for which there is not, and probably can never be, sufficient evidence. It is necessary, in response to this, to explain at once that talk of the communal philosophy of an ethnic group does not necessarily imply that the conceptions involved are entertained by all members of the group. What it means is that anybody thoughtfully knowledgeable about the culture will know that such conceptions are customary in the culture though s/he may not subscribe to it. The evidence for a communal philosophy is very much like that for the customs of a culture. In fact, in quite some cases customs are encapsulations of some aspects of a communal philosophy.

It is important, however, to note that a communal philosophy is the result of the pooling together over a considerable length of time the thoughts of individual thinkers. Propositions about, say, the constituents of human personality or the nature of time just don't materialize impromptu out of a cosmological bang, big, small, or medium. They emanate from human brains. In an oral tradition the names of the thinkers are often forgotten. This is not always so, however. In Ghana, for example, it is not at all rare for a proverb to be prefaced with the name of its author. Nor is it unusual for such sayings to evince originality and independence of mind. It goes without saying, therefore, that a communal philosophy is a gathering together of inputs from thinkers who may not have agreed on all points. And this, perhaps, accounts for the apparent inconsistencies that one sometimes notices in such bodies of belief.

Two lessons emerge. The first is this. There is nothing necessarily impeccable about a communal philosophy. It is the combining, in an almost imponderable process, of the opinions of fallible individuals. Moreover, these opinions are often only the most striking of the conclusions of the thinkers in question, preserved in the popular imagination in separation from the possibly complex and subtle reasonings that may have given rise to them. Such underlying argumentation is usually, although not invariably, forgotten. Yet it is this that gives a philosophy its profundity when it has any. It is, accordingly, the responsibility of contemporary African philosophers to delve beneath the communal beliefs to find their underlying reasons wherever possible. That is a necessary preparation for evaluation and reconstruction, two responsibilities complementary to the first.

Why is this a decolonizing program? It is because, ironically, the models of exposition in African philosophy established by writers like Tempels, who directly or indirectly worked for the colonization of the African mind, portrayed African communal philosophies as doctrinal givens, unquestionable for the African consciousness, though otherwise extremely questionable in themselves. An associated phenomenon, which is doubly ironic, is that in reaction to what is perceived as the colonial denial of philosophical capabilities to the African psyche, some contemporary African philosophers are apt to approach African communal philosophies in an almost warlike spirit. Any criticism of any aspect of these philosophies is regarded as a racial affront or, if it is by an African, as nothing short of a betrayal. This is a retrograde inflexibility for which, by and large, we have colonialism to thank.

This inflexibility is particularly unphilosophical because a philosophical thesis is a fundamental claim on the entire universe. It says what reality, whether social, physical or spiritual, is like. Thus, when the Akans, for example, say that the life principle of a human being is a speck of the divine substance, they cannot be understood to be characterizing Akan human beings alone. They are claiming that all human beings—Chinese, Indians, Africans, Americans, Europeans, etc.—are of that description. Then, for example, may not European or Chinese thinkers subject the thesis to a critical examination, provided that they take the trouble to inform themselves properly of its meaning and eschew any attitude of racial superiority?

To present African philosophy as an untouchable possession of Africans is to invite a touristic approach from its foreign audiences. If the philosophies may not be evaluated as false, they may not be evaluated as true either. In that case they might merely be noticed as cultural curiosities. This would aggravate a situation which already is not very healthy, for one has the distinct impression that many foreigners, particularly in the West, who have woken up to the recognition that there is such an animal as African philosophy do not as yet manifest any tendency to suspect that it is something from which they might conceivably have something to learn.

The second of the two lessons lately foreshadowed is that it is important to search out and study the thought of the individual indigenous philosophers who are contributors to the communal philosophies of our traditional societies. Such original thinkers are, in any case, worth studying in their own right. Studies of this kind, which are even more particularistic than studies of African communal philosophies, have the following decolonizing potential. They are likely to help erase the impression fostered in colonial and colonial-inspired treatments of African thought that Africa is lacking in individual thinkers of philosophic originality. An added bonus could be that the example of critical and reconstructive thinking on the part of our own indigenous philosophers might also help to wean some of our contemporary African philosophers from the merely narrative approach to the study of traditional African philosophy. The work that Professor Odera Oruka of the University of Nairobi has done in this direction in his *Sage Philosophy* therefore invites urgent continuation by as many workers in African philosophy in as many places on the continent as possible.

Since I mentioned customs at one point, let me repeat that, along with language, they constitute an essential resource in the study of a communal philosophy. Indeed language might, from one point of view, be seen as a kind of custom, a custom of symbolization. In the study of a culture, therefore, customs can be a veritable philosophical text; all of which suggests that if we want to correct any misapprehensions of a colonial origin about African philosophy, we ought to settle down to detailed investigations into particular African cultures.

This is not to say that there are no problems in this program of decolonization by particularization, so to speak. Take again the matter of language. Studies of the kind recommended involve essential uses of specific African languages. But there is a great multiplicity of languages in Africa, often inside a single African country. Thus if you take Akan, for example, it is spoken by only a minute proportion of the population of Africa. The question naturally arises whether the particularistic approach would not create blockages in inter-African philosophical communication, not to talk of philosophical communication further afield. This is an important question. The answer is as follows. To begin with, particularistic studies of various African peoples making such uses of particular African languages actually do exist already, especially in the religious and anthropological literature, and they cry for a decolonizing corrective. Furthermore, the philosophical interpretation of one African language may lead African philosophers speaking other African languages to make analogous inquiries into their own vernaculars with fruitful, if not necessarily corroborative, results. Actually, in my experience such studies have tended to converge more often than diverge.

Another circumstance which makes particularistic studies based on a given language not particularly impenetrable to non-speakers is that, as a rule, they consist of inferences from primary data, regarding which there is often little uncertainty, and on which, consequently, the non-insider can relatively safely depend. It is for this reason that non-speakers, whether they be African or non-African, can often evaluate controversies among African philosophers speaking the same language regarding the interpretation of aspects of their vernacular. For a quick illustration, recall the information that in Akan "to be" in the sense of "to exist" can only be expressed as *wo ho*, i.e., to be at some place. Suppose that two Akan philosophers, noting this, nevertheless disagree as to whether it follows that the notion of an immaterial substance is incoherent in the Akan language. I suggest that only a sense of logic is required in any other African or, for that matter, any member of the species homo sapiens, to deliberate on the issue.

It is worth emphasizing, besides, that African philosophers in our time cannot live by decolonization alone but also by the direct interrogation of reality. What is truth, goodness, freedom, time, causality, justice? What is the origin of the universe, the meaning of life, the destiny of the human soul (whatever it is)? What are the principles of correct reasoning? What are the best ways of acquiring knowledge? Grant that colonialism may have led to distorted accounts of the conceptions of our forefathers and foremothers on many of these issues. Grant that in some cases these issues may need recasting. Still, we contemporary Africans, too, have a duty to venture suggestions on these matters. In doing so we will, of course, have to take due account of our own heritage, as philosophers in other cultures routinely do. But we do not always need to call explicit attention to the cultural roots of our theories of reality. In any case, we would need to offer independent justifications for them. It may be said, then, that although at the present time we are still in an era of post-colonial reconstruction which calls for a large dose of decolonization, we ought not to be oblivious to the other imperatives of philosophical thinking. Decolonization, even as only one of our preoccupations, is not something that we will be doing forever in African philosophy. Of course, it will always make good sense in some contexts to speak, say, of the Bantu conception of something or other just as it still makes good sense for Western philosophers to talk of the ancient Greek conception of various things in historical and even analytical investigations, but such discussions will eventually not have quite the special urgency that they now have in African philosophy. The time will come when there would be, for the most part, no pressing need for the kind of particularism discussed above here.

For the time being, however, we in Africa have no option but to include in our projects, as a matter of urgency, a decolonizing program of pursuing the universal by way of the particular.

### The Philosophical Study of African Religions

In the first part of this essay I looked at the decolonization of African philosophy mostly in general terms. Now, I would like to examine decolonization with specific reference to the philosophical study of African religions. As you might expect from my advocacy of strategic particularism, my focus here will principally be on Akan religion as an example of African religions. I invite others to compare and contrast (where appropriate) their own perceptions of their indigenous religions. Religion is, indeed, an area in which there is a superabundance of characterizations of African thought in terms of inappropriate or, at best, only half-appropriate concepts. I shall examine concepts like creation out of nothing, omnipotence and eternity, and categorical contrasts such as the natural versus the supernatural and the physical versus the spiritual.

Africans nowadays frequently are said to be a profoundly religious people, not only by themselves but also by foreign students of their culture. This was not always so. Some of the early anthropologists felt that the concept of God, for example, was too sublime for the African understanding, granting that they had any understanding at all. The present situation in which indigenes as well as foreigners vie with one another to testify to the piety of the African mind is a remarkable reversal of earlier attitudes and prepossessions. There is virtual unanimity, in particular, on the report that Africans have a strong belief in the existence of God.

On all or virtually all hands it seems to be assumed that it speaks well of the mental capabilities of a people if they can be shown to have a belief in God, especially a God of a Christian likeness. Accordingly, the literature on African religions is replete with generalizations about African beliefs in the Almighty. In this discussion I want to start with a fairly extended look at the concept of God in the thought of the Akans of Ghana. Since this is the group to which I belong and in which I was raised, I hope I may be excused some show of confidence, although, of course, not dogmatism in making some conceptual suggestions about their thought. I will also try, more briefly, to make some contrasts between Akan thought and the thought of some other African peoples on the question of the belief in God, though this time more tentatively. It will emerge that not all African peoples entertain a belief in God and that this is, moreover, without prejudice to their mental powers.

Any cursory study of the thought and talk of the Akans will indeed reveal an unmistakable belief in a supreme being. This being is known under various names. I mention just a few here. *Nyame* is the word most often used for this being. It means something like "Absolute Satisfier." Another of his names is *Onyankopon*, which means, literally, "He Who Is Alone Great," a notion that reminds one of St. Anselm's "That Than Which a Greater Cannot Be Conceived," though this is not to assume conceptual congruence in other respects. There is also the name *Twediampon* ("He Upon Whom You Lean and Do Not Fall"). Cosmologically, perhaps, the most important name is *Oboade*, which, for the time being, I will translate as Creator. Frequently, the word *Nana* is added to either of the first two names. The word means grandparent, or ruler, or, in a more general sense, honored personage. In this context all these meanings are available, but often it is the grandfatherly connotation that is uppermost in the consciousness of people invoking the name.

Indeed, in the literature this grandfatherly appellation of God has often been emphasized by indigenous writers because some early European writers had suggested that the Akan (and, more generally, the African) God was an aloof God, indifferent to the fate of his creatures. These foreign observers even had the impression that this attitude of the supreme being was reciprocated by the Akans when they (the visitors) found among them no evidences of the worship of God, institutional or otherwise. In fact, however, the Akan have a strong sense of the goodwill of God; only this sentiment is not supposed, cosmologically speaking, to be manifested through *ad hoc* interventions in the order of nature.

The word "nature" is, perhaps, misleading in this context, in so far as it may suggest the complementary contrast of supernature. Here we come face to face with an important aspect of the cosmology of the Akans. God is the creator of the world, but he is not apart from the universe: He together with the world constitutes the spatio-temporal "totality" of existence. In the deepest sense, therefore, the ontological chasm indicated by the natural/supernatural distinction does not exist within Akan cosmology. When God is spoken of as creator we must remind ourselves that words can mislead. Creation is often thought of, at least in run-of-the-mill Christianity, as the bringing into existence of things out of nothing. The Akan God is certainly not thought of as such a creator. The notion of creation out of nothing does not even make sense in the Akan language. The idea of nothing can only be expressed by some such phrase as *se hwee nni ho*, which means something like "the circumstance of there not being something there." The word *ho* (there, at some place) is very important in the phrase; it indicates a spatial context. That of which there is a lack in the given location is always relative to a universe of discourse implicitly defined by the particular thought or communication. Thus, beholding a large expanse of desolate desert, an Akan might say that *hwee nni ho*. The meaning would be that there is a lack there of the broad class of things that one expects to find on land surface of that magnitude. The absolute nothingness entailed in the notion of creation out of nothing, however, scorns any such context. This abolition of context effectively abolishes intelligibility, as far as the Akan language is concerned.

But, it might be asked, does it not occur to the Akan that if God created the world, as s/he supposes, then prior to the act of creation there must have been nothing in quite a strict sense? The answer is that it depends at least on what one means by "create." In the most usual sense, creation presupposes raw materials. A carpenter creates a chair out of wood and a novelist creates fiction out of words and ideas. If God is conceived as a kind of cosmic architect who fashions a world order out of indeterminate raw material, the idea of absolute nothingness would seem to be avoidable. And this is, in fact, how the Akan metaphysicians seem to have conceived the matter. Moreover, *Oboade*, the Akan word that I provisionally translated as "creator," means the maker of things. *Bo* means "to make" and *ade* means "thing," but in Akan to *bo ade* is unambiguously instrumental; you only make something with something.

An almost automatic reaction to such an idea for many people is: If the "divine architect" fashioned the world out of some pre-existing raw material, then, however indeterminate it may have been, surely, somebody must have created it. But this takes it for granted that the concept of creation out of absolute nothingness makes sense. Since this is the question at issue, the reaction begs the question. If the concept of nothing in Akan is relative in the way explained, then obviously the notion of absolute nothingness will not make sense. The fundamental reason for this semantic situation in Akan is that, as pointed out in previous sections, in the Akan language existence is necessarily spatial. To exist is to *wo ho*, be at some location. So if God exists, he is *somewhere*. If nothingness excludes space, it has no accommodation in the Akan conceptual framework. On the other hand, if nothingness accommodates space, it is no longer absolute.

Of course, as suggested earlier, if a concept is incoherent within a given language, it does not necessarily mean that there is anything wrong with it, for it may be that the language in question is expressively inadequate. In the case of the concept of creation out of nothing, however, its coherence, even within English, is severely questionable. In English, the concept of "there is"—note the "there"—which is equivalent to "exists" is quite clearly spatial. Because the word "exists" does not wear its spatiality on its face, it has been possible in English to speak as if existence is not necessarily spatial without prohibitive implausibility. Besides, the maxim that *ex nihilo nihil fit* (Out of nothing nothing comes), which, ironically, is championed by Christian philosophers, such as Descartes, conflicts sharply with the notion of creation out of nothing. That nothing can come out of nothing is not an empirical insight; it is a conceptual necessity, just like the fact that two and two cannot add up to fifty. Thus to say that some being could make something come out of nothing is of the same order of incoherence as saying that some being could make two and two add up to fifty. Besides, as I have pointed out elsewhere, the causal connotation of creation is incompatible with the circumstance or rather, non-circumstance, of absolute nothingness. Causation makes sense only when it is, *in principle*, possible to distinguish between *post hoc* and *propter hoc* (i.e., between mere sequence and causal sequence). If there was one being and absolutely nothing besides him, then logically, that distinction was impossible. If so, the notion of causation collapses and with it that of creation.

So the notion of creation out of nothing would seem to be incoherent not only in Akan, but also absolutely. At least, the last reason given in evidence of its incoherence was an independent consideration, in the sense that it was independent of the peculiarities of Akan or English. It appealed only to a general logical principle. In fact, the conceptual difficulties in creation out of nothing have not been lost on religious thinkers, which accounts for the fact that it is not very unusual to find a sophisticated Christian metaphysician substituting some such rarefied notion as "the transcendental ground of existence" for the literal idea of creation even while cooperating with the generality of pious Christians in speaking of God as the creator. Another escape from the paradoxes of *ex nihilo* creation by some religious sophisticates, going far back into history, has been by way of emanationism. It might be worth remembering also in this connection that Plato's *demiurge* was an idea innocent of *ex nihilo* pretensions.

Be that as it may, it seems clear that the Akan supreme being is thought of as a cosmic architect rather than a creator out of nothing. The world resulting from the process of divine fashioning is conceived to contain all the potential for its development and bears all the marks of God's goodwill once and for all. In this scheme there are postulated various orders of beings. At the top of this hierarchy is God. Immediately below him are a host of extra-human beings and forces. Then come human beings, the lower animals, vegetation and the inanimate world, in that order. All these orders of being are believed to be subject to the universal reign of (cosmic) law. And the absence of any notion of creation out of nothing reflects the Akan sense of the ontological homogeneity of that hierarchy of existence.

Since I have mentioned inanimate things, I ought, perhaps, to dispose quickly of the allegation, often heard, that Africans believe that everything has life. The Akans, at least, are a counterexample. Some objects, such as particular rocks or rivers, may be thought to house an extra-human force, but it is not supposed that every rock or stone has life. Among the Akans a piece of dead wood, for example, is regarded as notoriously dead and is the humorous paradigm of absolute lifelessness. A graver paradigm of the same thing is a dead body. Thus the automatic attributions of animism to Africans manifests little empirical or conceptual wisdom.

To return to the subject of order. The strength of the Akan sense of order may be gauged from the following cosmological drum text.

> *Odomankoma*
> He created the thing
> "Hewer out" Creator
> He created the thing
> What did he create?
> He created Order
> He created Knowledge
> He created Death
> As its quintessence

I quote this from J. B. Danquah's *The Akan Doctrine of God*. The translation is Danquah's, and it incorporates a bit of interpretation, but it is, I think, accurate. What we need particularly to note is that to the Akan metaphysician, order comes first, cosmologically speaking. The stanza is a statement, above all else, to quote Danquah again, of "the primordial orderliness of creation."

This sense of order in phenomena is manifested at another level in the strong belief in the law of universal causation. There is an Akan saying to the effect that if nothing had touched the palm nut branches they would not have rattled (*se biribi ankoka papa a anka erenye kredede*). This is often quoted by writers on Akan thought as the Akan statement of universal causation. It is right as far as it goes, but there are more explicit formulations of the principle, such as one quoted by Gyekye: *Asem biara wo ne farebae*, which, literally, means everything has what brought it about. There is another formulation which, in addition to being more literal and explicit, is also more comprehensive. It says simply that everything has its explanation (*biribiara wo ne nkyerease*). The advantage of this formulation is that it discourages any impression that the sense of order under study is only conversant with mechanical causation. In Akan thought this kind of causation corresponds to only one kind of explanation; there are other kinds of explanation that are taken to evince the orderliness of creation (understanding creation, of course, in a quasi-demiurgic sense). These include psychological, rational, quasi-physical explanations and their various combinations of them. As one might expect, they correspond to the orders of being postulated in the Akan worldview.

To illustrate with a case which combines all these, suppose that an illness is interpreted as punishment from the ancestors for wrong conduct. There is here a cosmological dimension. The ancestors are conceived to be the departed spirits of erstwhile elders of our societies who live in a world analogous and contiguous to ours and work for the good of the living by watching over their morals. On this showing, they are both like and unlike the living. Like the living, they have an interest in morality of which they are, indeed, recognized as, in some ways, guardians. Moreover, in so far as any imagery is annexed to the conception of the ancestors, it is person-like. But unlike persons, they are not normally perceivable to the naked eye, and they can affect human life in superhuman ways for good or, in exceptional cases, as by the present hypothesis, for ill. The explanation involved here, then, is at once psychological, rational, mechanical, and quasi-physical. It is psychological because it is supposed that the hypothetical misconduct incurs the displeasure of the ancestors, which is a matter of mental dynamics. It is rational in conception, for the imagined punishment is viewed as a reformatory and deterrent measure, which, in principle, is a reasonable objective for enforcing morals. It has a "mechanical" aspect in that the illness being explained involves a physiological condition that will in many ways exhibit scenarios of physical causality. Finally, it is quasi-physical because, as pointed out, although the ancestors are psycho-physical in imagery, the manner of their operation is not fully constrained by the dynamic and associated laws familiar in day-to-day experience.

That the activities of beings, such as the ancestors, are not supposed to be completely amenable to "physical" laws is not to be taken to imply that they are regarded as contradicting them. What, in Western thought, are called physical laws in the Akan worldview are understood to govern the phenomena of one sphere of existence. But that understanding, as explained, also postulates another sphere of existence, which is believed to be governed, both internally and in interaction with the human sphere of existence, by laws different in some respects from physical or psychological laws and supplementary to them. Though generally Akans do not pretend to understand many aspects of the *modus operandi* of the beings and forces belonging to the superhuman sphere, they still view them as regular denizens of the cosmos. Moreover, there is no lack of "specialists" in Akan (and other African) societies who are supposed to have uncommon insights into the operations of such beings and enjoy expertise in communicating with them. Thus, the idea of ancestors punishing misbehavior evokes no sense of cosmological irregularity. On the contrary, it is perceived as exactly the kind of thing that might happen if people misbehave in certain ways.

Certain conceptual consequences flow immediately from these last considerations. To begin with, since all the orders of being are conceived to interact in a law-like manner, the natural/supernatural dichotomy will have no place in the Akan worldview, which reinforces our earlier remark on this issue made in a slightly different connection. Furthermore, the notion of a miracle does not make sense in this context, if a miracle is something supposed to happen contrary to the laws of "nature." Strange things may happen, of course, but in this system of thought, if they cannot be accounted for on the basis of the laws of the familiar world, they will be assumed to be accountable on some quasi-physical laws. This cosmological orientation seems to be not at all uncommon in Africa.

Yet, in the literature on African religions there are profuse references to the supposed African belief in the supernatural, which is frequently inspired by such things as ancestral veneration, almost standardly misdescribed as "ancestor-worship." Obviously, these misconceptualizations are the result of that superimposition of Western categories upon Akan thought-formations which is also the quintessence of conceptual colonization. Through education in colonial or neo-colonial circumstances, many Africans have come to assimilate these modes of thought and, in some cases, have internalized them so completely that they apparently can take great pride in propagating stories of the ubiquity of the supernatural in African thought. Perhaps, none of us Africans can claim total freedom from this kind of assimilation, but at least we can consciously initiate the struggle for conceptual self-exorcism.

Other aspects of the conceptual superimposition need to be noted. The beings I have, by implication, described as superhuman (but, note, not supernatural) are often called spirits. If the notion of spirits is understood in a quasi-physical sense, as they sometimes are, in narratives of ghostly apparitions even in Western thought, there is no problem of conceptual incongruity. But if the word "spirit" is construed, as so often happens, in a Cartesian sense to designate an immaterial substance, no such category can be fitted into the conceptual framework of Akan thought. The fundamental reason for this is to be found in the spatial connotation of the Akan concept of existence. Given the necessary spatiality of all existents, little reflection is required to see that the absolute ontological cleavage between the material and the immaterial will not exist in Akan metaphysics. Again, that Africans are constantly said to believe in spiritual entities in the immaterial sense can be ascribed to the conceptual impositions in the accounts of African thought during colonial times and their post-colonial aftermath.

It is, of course, an independent question whether the notion of an immaterial entity is intellectually viable. I will not pursue that question here. What is urgent, though, is to note certain further dimensions of the conceptual misdescriptions of African religions. One of the best-entrenched orthodoxies in the literature is the idea that Africans believe in a whole host of lesser gods or lesser deities. That many Akans have bought this story of a pantheon of "lesser gods" in their traditional religion must be due to a consistent forgetfulness of their own language when thinking about such matters. There is no natural way of translating that phrase into Akan. None of the names, as distinct from descriptions, for God in Akan has a plural. In any case, it is very misleading to call the superhuman beings and forces gods. Since the notion of a god, however diminutive, is intimately connected with religion, the use of that word in this context encourages the description of African attitudes to those entities as religious. Then, since Africans do often regard themselves as being in relationship with them, the stage is set for the inference that their life is completely pervaded by religion.

African scholars have not left it to foreigners alone to proclaim this image of African thought. Some of them have assumed eminent responsibilities in that direction. Thus, John Mbiti, for example, in his *African Religions and Philosophy*, has said things like, "Wherever the African is, there is his religion: he carries it to the fields where he is sowing seeds or harvesting a new crop; he takes it with him to the beer party or to attend a funeral ceremony…" or, "African peoples do not know how to exist without religion," or, "Religion is their whole system of being." At work here is an assimilation of African thought to Western categories.

At least as far as the Akans are concerned, it can be said that their attitude to those extra-human beings generally called minor gods in the literature is not really religious. On the contrary, it is utilitarian, for the most part. The powers in question are, as previously noted, a regular part of the resources of the world. If human beings understand how these powers function and are able to establish satisfactory relations with them, humans can exploit their powers to their advantage. One has, of course, to be circumspect because falling afoul of them could be dangerous. The way of establishing satisfactory relations with them is through those procedures that are often called rituals. But these rituals are not regarded as anything other than a method of making use of the super-human resources of the world. Because the powers that are called lesser gods are conceived to be, in some ways, person-like, the "rituals" often have a communicative component heavily laden with flattery. But the tactical character of the procedure is manifest in the fact that a so-called god who is judged inefficient, by reason, for example, of persistent inability to render help at the right time at the right place, is consigned to obsolescence by the permanent averting of attention. An attitude of genuine religious devotion cannot be thus conditional. Accordingly, it would seem inappropriate to call the "rituals" in question religious. Nor, for the same reason, can the procedures be called acts of *worship* unless the word is used in so broad a sense as to make the concept of worship no longer inseparably bound up with a religious attitude. That the attitude under discussion is not religious or that the procedures do not amount to worship does not imply a judgment that the people concerned fall short of some creditable practice; it simply means that the concepts of religion and worship have been misapplied to aspects of the given culture on the basis of un-rigorous analogies of a foreign inspiration. It would, in any case, be hasty to assume that there is anything necessarily meritorious about religious activities.

The Akans, in common with most other African peoples, nevertheless, do have a religious aspect to their culture. The question is as to its proper characterization. I would say that Akan religion consists solely in the unconditional veneration for God and trust in his power and goodness—i.e., in his perfection. This religion is, most assuredly, not an institutional religion, and there is nothing that can be called the worship of God in it. The insistence that any genuine belief in God must be accompanied with a practice of God-worship is simply an arbitrary universalization of the habits of religionists of a different culture. It is difficult, actually, to see how a perfect being could welcome or approve of such things as the singing of his praises.

Another significant contrast with other religions, particularly certain influential forms of Christianity, is that although God is held to be all-good, morality is not defined in Akan thought in terms of the will of God but rather in terms of human interests. Neither are procedures for the promotion of morality attached to Akan religion; they belong primarily to the home.

The inclusion of the attitudes and practices associated with the Akan belief in various superhuman beings and forces in the scope of Akan religion is an adulteration of the traditional religion that has exposed it quite severely to unconsidered judgment. It has helped to eclipse the religion in certain layers of the consciousness of the average educated Akan. The movement of thought has been as follows. When that overly inclusive view is taken of Akan religion, the supposed worship of the supposed gods looms so large in it that the whole religion becomes more or less identified with it. Thus it is that in Christian translation Akan religion is called *Abosomsom*, that is, the worship of stones. The same system of pious translation, by the way, called Christianity *Anyamesom*, that is, the worship of God. When, therefore ordinary educated Akans, brought up in Christianity, come to think that they have shed belief in the "lesser gods," they automatically see themselves as too enlightened for the traditional religion. Actually, the shedding of the traditional mind-cast is often only superficial. But let that pass. We were only concerned to illustrate what the uncritical assimilation of African categories by Western ones has done to an African self-image.

Let us return to the Akan God himself. An important question is how the Akans suppose that knowledge of him is obtained. In this connection there is an extremely interesting

Akan saying to the effect that no one teaches God to a child (*obi nkyere akwadaa Nyame*). This is sometimes interpreted to mean that knowledge of God is inborn and not the fruit of argumentation. But this is inconsistent with the implications of some of the names or descriptions for God in Akan.

One designation calls God *Ananse Kokroko*, meaning "The Stupendous Spider." The spider is associated with ingenuity in designing, and therefore the designation is clearly a metaphorical articulation of the notion of God as "The Great Designer." Similarly, Oguah, citing an Akan designation which calls God "The Great Planner," comments that we have here a hint of an argument which in Western philosophy is called a teleological argument. Oguah is, I think, right, and this shows that the Akans do think that reasoning is involved in the acquisition of the knowledge of the existence of God. If so, the maxim cited above is unlikely to be one that seeks to rule out the relevance of argument. Its most plausible interpretation is that the reasons for the belief in God are so obvious that even a child can appreciate them unaided.

In my own experience the previous interpretation tallies best with the reactions of the Akans not steeped in foreign philosophies that I have accosted from time to time on the justification of the belief in God. They have never refused the invitation to reason, though they have tended to be surprised that so obvious a point should be the object of earnest inquiry. The following type of argument has often been proffered:

> Surely, somebody must be responsible for the world. Were you not brought forth into this world by your parents? And were they not, in turn, by their parents, and so on? Must there not, therefore, be somebody who was responsible for everything?

Another type of argumentation that I have been supplied with is this:

> Every household has a father, and every town or country a king. Surely, there must be someone who rules the whole universe.

In this last connection a very common Akan saying comes to mind, namely, "God is King" (*Onyame ne hene*).

Regarding these arguments, no one can, or should, pretend that they are cogent pieces of reasoning, especially the last one. It is relevant to note that these arguments were deliberately solicited from ordinary Akans, not from their metaphysicians. But two points can be made; the second is of special significance for our discussion. First, if these arguments were sound, they would prove the conclusions advertised or something close. They would, that is, prove that there is a cosmic architect or ruler of the universe or something like that. This is much more than can be said for almost all the principal arguments for the existence of God in Western philosophy. These arguments also are such that, if they were sound, they would only prove some such being as a cosmic architect or governor. Yet, as a rule, there is, at the concluding point, an inconceivable leap to the affirmation of an *ex nihilo* Creator-God! On this point Hume's words should have been the last. He pointed out, in particular reference to teleological arguments, otherwise known as the argument from design, that even if granted valid, it would only prove a designer, not a creator [*ex nihilo*]. But "faith," even when it pretends to argue, is apparently stronger than logic, and the concluding unphilosophical leap remains a favorite exercise for some philosophers.

Second, and more importantly, the fact that even ordinary Akans are so willing to reason about the basic proposition of their religion demonstrates a rational attitude to religion which contrasts with the attitude which fundamentalist Christianity brought to many parts of Africa through the missionaries. Their key idea in this regard seems to have been "faith" as belief inaccessible to rational discussion. Many Africans have taken the idea to heart and have, in some cases, even been born again. If you ask them for the reason behind their preference for the new religion over the traditional one, the standard reply is that it is a matter of faith, not reason. I explained in previous sections why this answer is not sufficient. The foregoing discussion enables us to show also that this irrationality is uncharacteristic of the traditional outlook on religion. In fact, the notion of faith as belief without, and inaccessible to, reason is untranslatable into Akan except by an unflattering paraphrase—*gyidi hunu*—literally, "useless belief," is probably all that is available, unless one preferred a more prolix circumlocution, which would be something like *Gyidi a enni nkyerease*, that is, again literally, "belief without explanation." The pejorative connotation of the latter periphrasis, however, does not come through in the English version. Thus within Akan semantics it is difficult to validate the idea of faith being inhospitable to reason. In these circumstances one must admire the simplicity of the Christian solution to the problem of translating faith (in the non-rational sense) into Akan. They say simply *Gyidi*, which in genuine Akan means simply belief. Since this is patently inadequate, one must assume that the translators may have put their faith in *ad hoc* evangelical glosses. But it is also simple to see that decolonized thinking in religion must make short work of the evangelical talk of faith.

Let us once again return to the concept of God. Oguah advances the interesting claim that the Akan concept of God as the one who is alone great (*Onyankopon*) is the same as the concept of the greatest conceivable being or that than which nothing greater can be conceived, which formed the basis of Saint Anselm's ontological argument for the existence of God. In a formal sense this is correct, for an Akan believer cannot consistently concede the possibility of any being greater or even equal to God. However, this formal identity pales into insignificance when it is recalled that the Akan God is a cosmic architect while Anselm's is an *ex nihilo* creator. These two concepts are so different that the chances are that the ingenious saint would have considered the Akan concept quite atheistic. Accordingly, when we use the word God to translate *Nyame*, we must bear the disparity in connotation between this and the orthodox Christian concept of God firmly in mind.

This is particularly worth stressing in view of the tendency of many African writers on African religions, proud of their African identity, to suggest that their peoples recognize the same God as the Christians, since God is one. The origin of this tendency seems to me to be the following: Almost all these writers are themselves Christians, in most cases divines. Being scandalized by the opinion of some of the early European visitors to Africa that the African was too primitive to attain the belief in God unaided, they have sought to demonstrate that Africans discovered God on their own before a European or any foreigner, for that matter, set foot in Africa. However, since they themselves have been brought up to think that the Christian God is the one true God, it has been natural for them to believe that the God of their ancestors is, in fact, the same as the God of Christianity. Furthermore, they have been able to satisfy themselves that, in accepting Christianity, they have not fundamentally forsaken the religion of their ancestors. (Incidentally, in this respect, many African specialists of religious studies have differed from average African Christians, who, if they are Akans, would probably, at least verbally, declare traditional religion to be just *abosomsom*, the worship of stones.) Listen to what one famous African authority on African religions says:

> There is no being like "the African God" except in the imagination of those who use the term, be they Africans or Europeans. ... There is only one God, and while there may be various concepts of God, according to each people's spiritual perception, it is wrong to limit God with an adjective formed from the name of any race.

The writer was Professor Bolaji Idowu and the passage is cited in his *African Traditional Religion: A Definition*. Idowu was for many years Professor of Religions at the University of Ibadan and was in his retirement the Patriarch of the Methodist Church of Nigeria for some years. He is the author of, perhaps, the most famous book on the religion of the Yorubas, a book entitled *Olodumare: God in Yoruba Belief*. The Yorubas have a concept of God that is substantially identical with that of the Akans. This is confirmed by a careful study of direct descriptions of the Yoruba concept of God presented in the last mentioned book. In both cases what we have is a cosmic architect. But if this is so, it is an implausible suggestion that either the Yoruba or the Akan conception of God is just a different way of conceiving one and the same being as the God of Christianity. To see the fallacy clearly, consider that it is conceivable that God as a cosmic architect exists while an *ex nihilo* creator-God does not or cannot exist. Or, since Idowu's thesis is quite general, imagine that Spinoza, on the verge of excommunication from his synagogue on account of his view that God and nature are one, had sought to placate the authorities by proleptically taking a leaf out of Idowu's book and assuring them that God is one and that therefore they were all, after all, talking of the same being. The inevitable aggravation of tempers would, surely, have been blamable on no one but Spinoza himself. As it happened, the gentle metaphysician knew better than to attempt any such misadventure. But in pure logic, when Idowu tries to serve both *Olodumare* and the God of Christianity, he is embarking on a similar misadventure. More frankly, he is trying to eat his cake and have it too. The obvious lesson is that African thinkers will have to critically review both the conceptions—of God as *ex nihilo* creator and God as a cosmic architect—and choose one or none, but not both. Otherwise, colonized thinking must be admitted to retain its hold.

Since, by the present account, God is the beginning and the end of Akan religion, it may be useful to probe still further the Akan doctrine of God. In doing so, it will be important to bear in mind the point made at the end of the last paragraph about the attributes of the Akan God. I had argued that there are Akan expressions of God that will warrant saying that he is conceived to be omnipotent, omnibenevolent, omniscient, all-wise, and eternal. However, these attributes, especially omnipotence and eternity, must be understood only in a sense applicable to the type of being that a cosmic architect is. For example, the eternity of this being means simply that he has always existed and will always exist. The pressure that some Christian thinkers have felt to say that God is eternal in the sense of being timeless, that is, of not existing in time, is absent from the Akan mind. This pressure acts on some Christian minds because if God created everything out of nothing, then it might conceivably be wondered whether he did not create time also (however time may be conceived). And if he did, he can hardly be said himself to have been existing in time. It is well-known that Saint Augustine held that God created time along with everything else. (This great divine, by the way, was an African, but his mind was soaked in classical Roman culture. It is, indeed, speculated that his thought was not totally untouched by his African origins. But, if so, this particular doctrine was not one of the ways in which that fact may have manifested itself.)

Again, if we take the concept of omnipotence, we notice the same absence of the pressure to push it to transcendental proportions. The Akan God is omnipotent in the sense that he is thought capable of accomplishing any conceptually *well-defined* project. Thus, for example, he will not be supposed capable of creating a person who is at once six foot tall and not six foot tall, going by identical conventions of measurements. And this will not be taken to disclose a limitation on God's powers because the task description discloses no well-defined project. Perhaps, to many people this sounds unremarkable. But what about the following? It is apparent from one of the most famous Akan metaphysical drum texts that God is not supposed to be capable of reversing the laws of the cosmos. The question is whether the project is a coherent one. The answer from the point of view of the metaphysic in question is: "Of course, not!"

Here, then, is another illustration of formal identity amidst substantive disparities. Formally, both the Akan and the Christian may subscribe to the same definition of omnipotence as follows. "A being is omnipotent if and only if s/he or it can accomplish any well-defined project." Substantive differences, however, emerge when information is volunteered on both sides regarding the sorts of things that are or are not taken to be well-defined projects. It is interesting to note, in the particular case of omnipotence, that even this formal identity evaporates in the face of certain Christian interpretations of the concept. Omnipotence, for some Christian thinkers, means that God can do absolutely anything, including (as in the example mentioned above) creating a person who is both six foot tall and not six foot tall at the same time. On this showing, omnipotence implies the power to do even self-contradictory things. So powerful a Western Christian mind as Descartes was apparently attracted to this idea.

To be sure, the Akans are innocent of such a solecism. But they are not free from the intellectual difficulties that have plagued the Christian doctrine of omniscience, omnibenevolence, omnipotence and unlimited wisdom. If God has all these qualities, couldn't he have prevented the abundance of evil in the world? And ought he not to have done so? This is the problem of evil. In discussing it one thing that will become clear is that the communal philosophy of a traditional society need not always display unanimity, contrary to the impression fostered by certain colonial-type studies of African life and thought.

It is sometimes suggested that the problem does not really arise in Akan thought. Helaine Minkus, an American researcher who went and lived among the Akwapim Akans, learnt their language and studied their philosophy, advances a view of this sort in her "Causal Theory in Akwapim Akan Philosophy":

> God's attribute of transcendence and the concomitant belief that he has delegated power to the other agents that more directly interact with human beings pragmatically diminish His omnipotence. The other agents are treated in practice as if endowed with an independent ability to act. ... The postulation of a great number of beings empowered to affect events, joined with the acceptance of evil as necessarily co-existing with good from creation obviates the problem of evil so burdensome to those monotheistic theologians who define the Supreme Being as both omnipotent and totally benevolent and attempt a reconciliation of these qualities with the existence of evil.

Minkus talks here of the pragmatic diminution of God's omnipotence. But this represents a dilemma rather than a dissolution. If the diminution of omnipotence is only "pragmatic," God, as the ultimate source of the powers delegated to the "other agents," remains ultimately in charge, and the original problem, equally ultimately, remains. If, on the other hand, the diminution is real, this contradicts the well-attested postulate of omnipotence in Akan cosmology. Is the contradiction a feature of Minkus's exposition or of the Akan system expounded? I shall return to this question below.

Interestingly, in an earlier exposition of Akan thought Busia had shifted the responsibility for evil from God to the "other agents" not pragmatically but positively. He remarks,

> [T]he problem of evil so often discussed in Western philosophy and Christian theology does not arise in the African concept of deity. It is when a God who is not only all-powerful and omniscient but also perfect and loving is postulated that the problem of the existence of evil becomes a philosophical hurdle. The Supreme being of the African is the Creator, the source of life, but between him and man lie many powers and principalities good and bad, gods, spirits, magical forces, witches to account for the strange happenings in the world.

Gyekye quotes this passage in his *Essay* and points out that if God is omnipotent, the question still arises why he does not control the "lesser spirits." This, he rightly concludes, shows that the problem of evil is not obviated. Gyekye's own account of the Akan solution of the problem of evil, which, for him, is a real problem in Akan philosophy, is that

> [t]he Akan thinkers, although recognizing the existence of moral evil in the world, generally do not believe that this fact is inconsistent with the assertion that God is omnipotent and wholly good. Evil, according to them, is the result of the exercise by humans of their freedom of the will with which they were endowed by the Creator, Oboadee.

On Gyekye's account, the Akan thinkers in question advocated a solution to the problem of evil which is also canvassed by some Western thinkers and is known as the "free-will defense." Gyekye is certainly right in seeing this solution in Akan thought. But Akan sources also reveal other solutions. Before noticing some of them, let us note two things with regard to the free-will defense, as it relates to moral evil. First, it does not provide a satisfactory answer to the question why God does not intervene to stop or forestall evil acts when they are planned. This is, of course, different from the idea that God could have guaranteed *ab initio* that human beings made only right choices. The usual reply to the suggested intervention is that it would destroy the free will of humans, but that reply does not appear to be plausible. Even human beings are sometimes able to intervene by force or by persuasion to stop the evil designs of others, without affecting their free will. In the abstract, countless smooth ways are conceivable by which God might forestall, counteract or neutralize the evil acts that humans might use their free will to contemplate. Possibly, there might be something wrong with this hypothesis; but clearly, it would not be because of any threat to free will. Second, this solution does not begin to deal with physical evil.

However, the problem of physical evil might, theoretically, be tackled by Akan advocates of the free-will defense with only a little elaboration on the remark of Busia quoted above. They might simply argue that the "principalities, good and bad, spirits, gods," etc., rather than God, are responsible for physical evil, or in Busia's phrase, "for the strange happenings in the world." On this supposition, these happenings would be the result of the exercise, by those beings, of the free will "with which they were endowed by the Creator." In Western philosophy, by the way, the same idea occurred to Saint Augustine, who debited Satan and his cohorts with a lot of the physical evil in the world, a maneuver which has recently been exploited by some highly sophisticated apologists. In the face of these claims, one can but await probative evidence.

Meanwhile, we should note another Akan position on the question of evil which is evident in the quotation from Minkus (which she does not separate from her theory, on behalf of the Akans, of the pragmatic diminution of God's omnipotence). Minkus attributes to the Akans "the acceptance of evil as necessarily co-existing with good from creation." What is proposed here is not just the semantic point that you cannot talk of good if the possibility of the contrast with evil did not exist, but rather the substantive cosmological claim that the components of existence which we describe as good could not possibly exist without those components we call evil. That the Akans do actually entertain this thought is attested to by a common saying among them. It is, indeed, one of the commonest sayings of the Akans, "If something does not go wrong," they say, "something does not go right" (*se biribi ansee a, biribi nye yie*).

However, even if it is granted that good cannot exist without evil, that still does not amount to a theodicy, for it does not follow that the quantity of evil in the world does not go beyond the call of necessity. But there is another Akan saying that seems to suggest exactly this. The Akans delight in crediting their maxims to animals, and in this instance the epigrammatic surrogate is the hawk. It is said: "The hawk says that all that God created is good" (*osansa se nea Onyame yee biara ye*). The sense here is not that all is good to a degree that could conceivably be exceeded but rather that all is maximally good. Again, the hawk is not trying to fly in the face of the palpable facts of evil in the world; what it is saying is that the evil, though it is evil, is unavoidably involved in the good and is ultimately for the best—a sentiment that would have warmed the heart of Leibniz, author, in Western philosophy, of the maxim that this is the best of all possible worlds.

But how do we know that? Possibly, because of the difficulty of this question the Akans, or at any rate, some of them, do not seem to have sustained this cosmic optimism indefinitely, and there is evidence of another approach to the problem of evil which seeks to dissolve it by foregoing the claim of the total omnipotence of God. This brings us back to the pragmatic diminution of omnipotence spoken of by Minkus. But this time the diminution is real, not pragmatic. So too is the possibility of inconsistency in the traditional thought of the Akans on this subject. Though in the context of cosmological reflection, they maintain a doctrine of unqualified omnipotence, in connection with issues having a direct bearing on the fate of humankind on this earth, such as the problem of evil; they seem to operate with a notion of the power of God implying rather less than absolute omnipotence. That power is still unique in its extent, but it is conceptually not altogether unlike that of a human potentate. Indeed, correspondingly, God himself comes to be thought of on the model of a father who has laid well-intentioned plans for his children which are, however, sometimes impeded not only by their refractory wills but also by the grossness of the raw materials he has to work with. In conformity with this way of seeing God, a popular Akan lyric cries: "God descend, descend and come and take care of your children" (*Onyame sane, sane behwe wo mma*). The apparent inconsistency in this dual conception of God and his powers in the Akan communal philosophy may possibly be due to its diversity of authorship; but, on the other hand, it may well be a real inconsistency harbored in identical Akan minds. Actually, a similar inconsistency is evident in some Christian thinking on the same problem.

Be that as it may, the position in question is approvingly expounded by J. B. Danquah as the Akan solution to the problem of evil. I beg permission to quote from Danquah *in extenso*.

> What, then, is the Akan solution to the fact of physical pain in man's animate experience? On the Akan view, we could only regard this as a difficulty if we lost sight of the fundamental basis of their thought, namely, that Deity does not stand over against his own creation, but is involved in it. He is, if we may be frank, "of it." If we postulate, as the Christians do, that the principle that makes for good "in this world," *Nyame* or God, stands over against the community ... and if we postulate again that the aforementioned principle is omnipotent, and is also responsible as creator of this world, the existence of physical evil or pain ... becomes an insoluble mystery. ... It is quite otherwise if we deny that the principle is omnipotent but is itself a "a spirit striving in the world of experience with the inherent conditions of its own growth and mastering them" at the cost of the physical pain and evil as well as the moral pain or disharmony that stain the pages of human effort. ... That is to say, in Akan language, where the Nana, the principle that makes for good, is himself or itself a participant in the life of the whole ... physical pain and evil are revealed as natural forces which the Nana, in common with others of the group, have to master, dominate, sublimate or eliminate.

This must remind one of John Stuart Mill, who was constrained by the problem of evil to resort to the concept of a limited God.

Danquah is not quite right in seeming to think that the view just noted is the one and only solution to the problem of evil in Akan thought. Whether by way of inconsistency or doctrinal fecundity among Akan thinkers, there is, as shown above, a diversity of thought on the problem. This discussion, then, demonstrates a vitality of philosophical thought in an African traditional society that the generality of colonial studies of African thought, in tending to give the impression of monolithic unanimity, has tended to obscure. It also shows another thing. It shows, in view of the repeated examples of philosophical convergences, that although it is the hallmark of decolonized thinking to be critically cognizant of the differences between African thought and its Western counterpart in its various forms, this is without prejudice to the possibilities of parallels in intellectual concerns and even doctrinal persuasion. This, it need hardly be added, can be a basis for fruitful exchange/interchange between African and Western (and, presumably, also Oriental) philosophy.

The reference to philosophical diversity early in the last paragraph is worth exploring at least briefly. The multiplicity of philosophic options is in evidence not only within the Akan tradition, but also across the African continent. Thus, it is not to be taken for granted that the Akan doctrine of a basically demiurgic God is universal in Africa. Based on the evidence of studies such as Harry Sawyerr's *God: Ancestor or Creator?* and Kofi Asare Opoku's *West African Traditional Religion*, it might be conjectured that it is widespread in West Africa. On the other hand, if Mbiti is right, this does not apply to certain other parts of Africa. The latter observes that the "concept of creation *ex nihilo* is ... reported among the Nuer, Banyarwanda and Shona, and undoubtedly a careful search for it elsewhere is likely to show that there are other peoples who incorporate it into their cosmologies." As regards the Banyarwanda, Maquet has written as follows:

> The world in which men are placed and which they know through their senses was created *ex nihilo* by *Imana*. The Ruanda word, *kurema*, means to produce, to make. It is here rendered "to create" because our informants say that there was nothing before *imana* made the world. This belief concerning the origin of the material world is universal and clear. To any question on this point, the answer is ready.

This account, if it is right, together with our previous findings, shows that not all traditional Africans think alike about God. It would seem that the Banyarwanda think more like orthodox Christians than like the traditional Akans. Actually, though, Maquet's account is not unproblematic. He says, for example, that *Imana*, the God of the Banyarwanda, "is non-material. His action influences the whole world; but Ruanda is his home where he comes to spend the night."

How does a non-material being spend the night, and in physical environs, such as Ruanda? Presumably, the idea is that a non-material being can sometimes materialize itself, i.e., manifest itself in a material guise. But this involves a category mistake not unlike that of supposing that the square root of minus one might be able to dance calypso from time to time. Moreover it is as full-blooded a logical inconsistency as ever there was. Is the present incarnation of that inconsistency Maquet's or the Banyarwanda's? While the question remains open, confidence in Maquet's report of the belief in *ex nihilo* creation among the Banyarwanda cannot be limitless, though it cannot be discounted out of hand.

According to Okot p'Bitek, the religious thought of both the Akans and the Banyarwanda is in vast contrast to that of the Luo of Uganda. For him the Central Luo do not entertain any belief in a Supreme, or, as he phrases it, High God. They do not even have truck with the concept of such a being, nor does the notion of creating or even molding the world make sense within their conceptual framework. In two books, namely, *African Religions in Western Scholarship* and *Religion of the Central Luo*, he argues with intriguing illustrations that "the idea of a high God among the Central Luo was a creation of the missionaries."

If truth be told, Okot p'Bitek was the true pioneer of conceptual decolonization in African philosophy. His *African Religions in Western Scholarship* might well have been sub-titled "The Decolonization of African Religions." He is an interesting exception to the practice among African writers of endeavoring to prove to the world that Africans had, by their own efforts, reached a concept of God essentially identical with the God of Christianity before the arrival of the missionaries. The general assumption among these writers, as I pointed out earlier, has been that it is a glorious achievement for a culture to be able to arrive, without outside help, at the belief in a God who created the world out of nothing. P'Bitek had no such assumption. He was a skeptic, and found nothing necessarily creditable in such a belief. He thus had no special joy at the prospect of it being demonstrated that the Central Luo were original true believers. It is, of course, open to his critics to argue that, in writing as he did, he was foisting his own unbelief upon his people. There is, certainly, no substitute for an objective and conceptually critical examination of his account of Luo religion. That would, in itself, be an admirable exercise in conceptual decolonization. For my part, given the ease and frequency with which Western categories of thought have been superimposed on African thought, I am inclined to suspect him innocent until proven guilty.

According to p'Bitek, then, the Central Luo believe in a whole host of forces or powers called, in their language, *jogi* (plural of *jok*), each independent of the rest. These *jogi* are regarded as responsible for particular types or patterns of happenings. Some of them are chiefdom *jogi* who are supposed to see to the welfare of particular groups of people. Others are hostile. For example, *jok kulu* causes miscarriage, *jok rubanga* causes tuberculosis of the spine, etc. Even the supposed power of a witch to cause harm is called a *jok*. Some *joks* may be used against other *joks*, but no one *jok* dominates all. This is far cry, indeed, from the Christian religious ontology which postulates an omnipotent creator *ex nihilo* or from even the Akan system with its divine architect who is "alone great."

Substantiating his assertion that the idea of a high God among the Luo was the invention of the Christian missionaries, p'Bitek recounts the following incident in *African Religions and Western Scholarship*. I have quoted it elsewhere in a similar connection but I cannot forebear to quote it again in the present context, as it furnishes a perfect paradigm of conceptual imposition in perfect drama:

> In 1911, Italian Catholic priests put before a group of Acholi elders the question "Who created you?"; and because the Luo language does not have an independent concept of *create* or *creation*, the question was rendered to mean "Who moulded you?" But this was still meaningless, because human beings are born of their mothers. The elders told the visitors that they did not know. But we are told that this reply was unsatisfactory, and the missionaries insisted that a satisfactory answer must be given. One of the elders remembered that, although a person may be born normally, when he is afflicted with tuberculosis of the spine, then he loses his normal figure, he gets "moulded." So he said "Rubanga is the one who moulds people." This is the name of the hostile spirit which the Acholi believe causes the hunch or hump back. And instead of exorcising the hostile spirits and sending them among pigs, the representatives of Jesus Christ began to preach that Rubanga was the Holy Father who created the Acholi.

Disentangling African frameworks of thought from colonial impositions, such as this, is an urgent task facing African thinkers, especially, philosophers, at this historical juncture. Clarifying African religious concepts should be high on the agenda of this kind of decolonization.

# SOCIAL ANTHROPOLOGY AND COLONIALISM

I first met a number of Western scholars at Oxford University in 1960. During the very first lecture in the Institute of Social Anthropology, the teacher kept referring to Africans or non-Western peoples as barbarians, savages, primitives, tribes, etc. I protested; but to no avail. All the professors and lecturers in the Institute, and those who came from outside to read papers, spoke the same insulting language.

In the Institute Library, I detested to see such titles of books and articles in the learned journals as *Primitive Culture, Primitive Religion, The Savage Mind, Primitive Government, The Position of Women in Savage Societies, Institutions of Primitive Societies, Primitive Song, Sex and Repression in Savage Societies, Primitive Mentality,* and so on.

In this book I trace the study of African religions by Western scholars from the classical times [in European history] to the [1970s]. Two major conclusions are reached. First, that whereas different schools of social anthropology may quarrel bitterly over *methods*, they may all share the same view that the population of the world is divisible into two: one, their own, *civilized*, and the rest, *primitive*. The second conclusion is that Western scholars have never been genuinely interested in African religions *per se*. Their works have all been part and parcel of some controversy or debate in the Western world....

. . .

Hitherto, social anthropology has been the study of non-Western societies by Western scholars to serve Western interests. Social anthropology has not only been the handmaiden of colonialism in that it analyzed and provided important information about the social institutions of colonized peoples to ensure efficient and effective control and exploitation, it has also furnished and elaborated the myth of the "primitive" which justified the colonial enterprise. The study of African religions was part and parcel of this exercise.

From the fifteenth century onwards, the most aggressive civilization embarked upon a program more ambitious than any previously known, of exploiting the resources and inhabitants of the entire globe. In 1496 John Cabot, the "discoverer" of Newfoundland, was given a royal patent by Henry VII to "subdue, conquer and possess" the foreign lands which he might discover. In 1501 a royal patent was granted to Bristol merchants to settle colonies in newly "discovered" lands. The Bahamas was annexed by Sir Henry Gilbert in 1578. By 1562 John Hawkins had ravaged Sierra Leone and sailed away with a cargo of enslaved Africans.

Karl Marx wrote, "The discovery of gold and silver in America, the extirpation, enslavement and entombment in mines of the aboriginal population, the beginning of the conquest and looting of the East Indies, the turning of Africa into a warren for the commercial hunting of black skins, signaled the rosy dawn of capitalist production. ... The colonial system ripened, like a hothouse. ... The treasures captured outside Europe by undisguised looting, enslavement and murder, floated back to the mother country and were turned into capital."[2]

In his *First Will and Testament*, 1877, Cecil Rhodes left all his wealth "to and for the establishment, promotion and development of a Secret Society, the true aim and object whereof shall be the extension of British rule throughout the world ... and especially the occupation by British settlers of the entire Continent of Africa, the Euphrates, the islands of Cyprus, the whole of South America and Canada, the Islands of the Pacific not heretofore possessed by Great Britain, the whole of Malay Archipelago, the seaboard of China and Japan, the ultimate recovery of the United States of America as an integral part of the British Empire."[3]

Christopher Dawson has argued that to present the history of this European expansion as a process of imperialistic aggression and economic exploitation was not enough. Aggression and exploitation, he said, were not new in world history. "For side by side with the natural aggressiveness and the lust for power and wealth which are so evident in European history, there were also new spiritual forces driving Western man towards a new destiny." The spiritual force was provided by the Christian faith which saw humanity as born under a curse, enslaved by the dark powers of cosmic evil and sinking even deeper under the burden of its own guilt. "Only by the way of the Cross and by the grace of the crucified Redeemer was it possible for men to extricate themselves from the *massa damnata* of unregenerate humanity and escape from the wreckage of the doomed world."[4]

But it was a Papal Bull which authorized the opening of the slave market in Lisbon in the first decade of the sixteenth century. The Christian English Parliament passed an act legalizing the purchase of slaves in 1565. Till the end of the Middle Ages monasteries and ecclesiastics possessed slaves, and as late as 1542 a pope defended their right to do so.[5] Eugene Stock confessed, "It is a humiliating fact that for more than two centuries England was the chief trading nation. She did not indeed begin the detestable traffic. It was the Portuguese who first kidnapped negroes and carried them across the Atlantic to provide labor for the early settlers in the New World."[6]

Attempt have been made to present the activities of the humanitarians as the key to the abolition and the ending of the slave trade and slavery. But, as Eric Williams has convincingly argued, it was not philanthropic ideals but changing economic conditions that ended the institution. The importance of the humanitarians has been seriously misunderstood and grossly exaggerated.[7]

The wholesale murder of the indigenous peoples of the Americas and Australia and the Khoisan to give way to European settlers and the enslavement of Africans makes it difficult to understand the great Western mission to show mankind "the way of the Cross and the grace of the Crucified Redeemer."

The foundation of social anthropology as an independent study goes back to the beginning of the nineteenth century. The Société Ethnologique de Paris was founded in 1839. Four years later the Ethnological Society was formed in London.[8] The American Ethnological Society was constituted in New York in 1844. The colonial powers of the time were forced by practical interests in the conditions of life among their subject peoples to carry out studies of those conditions. Ethnological investigations "were felt to be of daily increasing importance in relation to the commercial and maritime interests, the missionary enterprise and many other objects of practical utility."[9] Germany became a colonial power later, and it was only then that the need to carry out researches in German colonies was felt in that country, and the fact that she was a late starter acted as a spur to German scholars.[10]

The nineteenth century anthropologists had three major roles to play:

(a) Solving the problem of the remnants of aboriginal peoples in America and Australia, and the fate of the freed slaves;
(b) Tackling the problem of subduing and exploiting the vigorous societies such as were found in Africa; and
(c) Justifying the colonial system by elaborating the myth of the "primitive."

We note that the moving spirits behind the foundation of the Société Ethnologique in France were the natural philosophers, Edward and his brother Amedee Thiery, who were primarily interested in the intensive study of the characters and aptitudes of the races of mankind. And in Britain many of the earliest anthropologists were practicing doctors, and members of philanthropic societies. Dr. Hodgkin, in whose house the foundation meeting of the Ethnological Society was held, was also a founder member of the Aborigines Protection Society. These men were moved by their concern for the fate of the defeated remnants of the aborigines and the predicament of the emancipated slaves. Philanthropic agencies such as the Negro Emancipation Society and the British Colonization Society used the information adduced by these scholars as best they could.[11]

The contribution of social anthropology to colonial administration has been fully discussed and acknowledged.[12] In their loyal address to the King of England, the Royal Anthropological Institute of Great Britain and Ireland stated, "From the earliest days of the Institute problems relating to the culture and welfare of the less advanced peoples of Your Empire have been the object of continued investigation both by the Institute and by its individual Fellows."[13] When the Board of Anthropology was established at Cambridge in 1904, Sir Richard Temple laid great stress on the importance of anthropology for those who were destined to serve in the colonies. The necessary knowledge, he said, could not be acquired by simply living among a people of different culture; it needed a habit of intelligently examining them, and the cultivation of such a habit as well as the accumulation of scientific knowledge was what he hoped would be encouraged in the University.[14]

Is there a place for social anthropology in an African university? In my opinion the answer is no. The departments of social anthropology in African universities were camping grounds for Western anthropologists. African universities can ill-afford to maintain these bases. Africans have no interests in, and cannot indulge in perpetuating the myth of the "primitive."

The study of African peoples and their culture is the task of the whole university. What Western social anthropologists purported to study, in the interest of their countries, will be covered by the humanities departments: history, geography, economics, languages, literature, etc., in the interest of African development. The department of religious studies must concentrate more on the beliefs of African peoples. It must become a true center for research rather than continuing to be a monastery for training priests of foreign religions.

The African scholar has two clear tasks before him. First, to expose and destroy all false ideas about African peoples and culture that have been perpetuated by Western scholarship. Vague terms such as *Tribe*, *Folk*, *Non-literate* or even innocent-looking ones such as *Developing*, etc., must be subjected to critical analysis and thrown out or redefined to suit African interests. Second, the African scholar must endeavor to present the institutions of African peoples as they really are. Western scholars had to justify the colonial system, hence the need for the myth of the "primitive." The African scholar has nothing of the sort to justify. But he [or she] must guard against overreacting in the face of the arrogance and insults of Western scholarship. This is already happening in the field of religious studies where African scholars now claim that African deities have all the attributes of the Christian God. The African scholar is called upon to participate fully in nation building, and he can best do this by presenting the *truth* about Africa.

## WHAT IS TRIBE?

Although social anthropology has been described as the study of man and his works, in Western scholarship it has been, until very recently, the study of the so-called "tribal" peoples, and has known very little interest in Western industrialized societies. As Joseph H. Greenberg has commented, in practice social anthropology has concentrated on "primitive" and "pre-literate" peoples and "many of the characteristics of cultural anthropological methodology and theory have resulted from this preoccupation. The basic technique in field study, by observation and participation and verbal interviews of relatively small groups typically organized on a tribal basis." Robert Redfield stated, "We look from our position, that of the anthropological investigator, out, to, and inside of those other people, over there, doing things and thinking thoughts that we seek to understand. We are extrospective not introspective."[15]

[...Here,] we must try to discover the meaning, if any, of the word "tribe" as used in Western scholarship, and to discuss its relevance in African development. Lewis wrote that, in general usage, the word tribe is taken to denote a primary aggregate of peoples living in a primitive or barbaric condition under a chief. He is not happy with what he calls the unnecessarily moralistic overtones that this usage implies, and suggests that it could be avoided or minimized by the use of the expression "tribal society."[16]

Henry Maine had contrasted the territorial foundations of the so-called "modern state" with what he considered to be the kinship basis of "tribal" societies. He wrote, "From the moment when a tribal community settles down finally upon a definite space of land, the land begins to be the basis of society in place of kinship.... For all groups of men larger than the family, the land on which they live tends to become the band of union between them at the expense of kinship, even more and more vaguely conceived."[17] Lewis rejects this, and calls for an entirely different approach.[18] What is significant, he argues, is not the presence or absence of particular principles of social grouping, but the form, shape and design of society itself. Thus while taking into account the implications of such synonyms as "simple society," "pre-industrial society" or "folk society," a satisfactory characterization of "tribal society" must therefore be that of form rather than content; and, for him (following Wilson and Wilson, *Nyakusa*, 1945), the most useful criterion is that of *scale*. He writes, "Ideally tribal societies are small in scale, are restricted in spatial and temporal range of their social, legal and political relations, and possess a morality, religion, and world-view of corresponding dimensions."[19]

The question arises, where were such simple societies in Africa? Comparing the remnants of the so-called Australian Aborigines and the [indigenous peoples of the Americas] with African societies, Meyer Fortes remarked, "A tribe of ten thousand Tswana, two hundred thousand Bemba, or half a million Ashanti cannot run their social life on exactly the same pattern as an Australian horde.... In Africa one comes across economies whereas in Australia or part of North America one meets only housekeeping, one is confronted with government whereas in societies of smaller scale one meets social control; with organized warfare, with complicated legal institutions, with elaborate forms of public worship and systems of belief comparable to the philosophy and theological systems of literate civilizations."[20] In the opinion of this British writer there are few truly isolated societies in Africa, which he does not mention. But we note that he still refers even to the examples he gives as "tribes." Why is this?

The Nilotic peoples are found in western Ethiopia, northern Uganda, eastern Congo (Kinshasa), western Kenya and northern Tanzania. They are not referred to as a nation, because, although they have certain institutions in common, they do not form one political unit. Writers have used the term "tribe" to refer to the different groups of Nilotes. In British anthropology the term tribe has acquired a restricted technical meaning, that is, the widest territorially defined politically independent unit. At the turn of the century Acoliland was divided into thirty politically independent units.[21] But these have not been called "tribes." They were known as "chiefdoms." It was the new political unit set up by the British colonial administration which was labeled Acoli District, which came to be known as the Acoli "tribe."[22]

In his study of the Nuer, Evans-Pritchard found that although this chiefless Nilotic people, numbering 200,000, have a common name, a common language, and a common culture, they were divided into distinct political units. He defined "tribe" as the largest territorial unit within which members of the tribe would unite against external aggression and settle internal differences by arbitration. The Nuer then are divided into a number of "tribes." Likewise in his short paper on the Kenya Luo, he equates the administrative locations with "tribe." He writes, "At the present time Luoland is divided into a number of administrative locations. These locations correspond approximately with old tribal areas of the Luo, with the exception of Karachuonyo, Mumbo, Kabondo which comprised a single tribe, as did north and south Gem, north and south Uganya, west and east Kano." According to this analysis there are twenty-seven "tribes" in Luoland.[23]

Lucy Mair commented, "If one is using the word in this way it could be defined that the tribe is a politically organized subdivision of a wider ethnic or cultural unit. This would be in accordance with the usage by which the Tswana are said to be subdivided into eight tribes, each with its own chief. The word could also be applied to the subdivisions of the six million Ibo [Igbo] of Nigeria, and in many other cases."[24] This is the typical talk of Western anthropologists who are colonially oriented and refuse to understand the meaning of African independence. Even during the colonial period, the thirty independent chiefdoms in Acoliland were regrouped into six "countries," each with a civil servant chief, appointed and paid by the colonial administration. Today, the affairs of Acholi District are run by the District Council. Following the revolution which overthrew the Kabaka of Buganda, the former Buganda Kingdom is now divided into four districts, and as in all the districts of the Republic of Uganda, the affairs of the districts are run by a District Council. There are no politically organized subdivisions. In short, no "tribes" as defined by Western scholars.

The term "tribe" turns out to have no definite meaning, in that it refers to no specific unit in Africa. But this term has come to mean something very different in Africa itself. During the civil war in Nigeria the Ibo [Igbo] were frequently referred to as a "tribe," and their struggle to break away from the Federation dubbed "tribalism." Corrupt practices by government officers and others, such as giving employment not through merit but by kinship relations, or concentrating public utilities such as hospitals, schools, etc., in one's own home area, which have been known throughout history and in all corners of the world, are described as "tribalism" in Africa. And, even normal demands for equitable distribution of the national wealth, in terms of areas, have been called "tribalism." Abner Cohen has argued, "The phenomenon called 'tribalism' in contemporary Africa is the result, not of ethnic groups disengaging themselves from one another after independence, but increasing interaction between them within the context of the new political situation. It is the outcome, not of conservatism, but a dynamic socio-cultural change brought about by the new cleavages and new alignments of power within the framework of the new state."[25] In my opinion, it is misleading and confusing to analyze the social ills of Africa, which are, in any case, universal, in terms of the so-called phenomenon of "tribalism." And, for a clearer understanding of our problems, it is suggested that the term "tribe" ought to be dropped from sociological vocabulary.

But, an even more important reason for dropping the term "tribe" is that it is an insult. It means people living in primitive or barbaric conditions and each time it is used, as in the sentence, "I am a Kikuyu [Gikuyu] by tribe," the implication is that the speaker is a Kikuyu who lives in a primitive or barbaric condition. And when we read of "tribal law," "tribal economics" or "tribal religion," Western scholars imply that the law, economics or religion under review are those of primitive or barbaric peoples.

This is what was in the mind of Lewis when he wrote, "But the concept ['tribe'] will remain useful not only for understanding the way in which tribal societies have changed, and are changing, in the modern world but also as a theoretical construction in the comparative study of social systems and institutions. Even when all truly tribal societies have disappeared, the fact that under certain conditions certain combinations of institutions have provided the basis for a viable social system at some point in man's history is of the utmost importance to the student of society."[26] It is also the same idea which is at the root of the so-called phenomenon of "detribalization."

Western scholarship sees the world as divided into two types of human society: one, their own, civilized, great, developed; the other, the non-Western peoples, uncivilized, simple, undeveloped. One is modern, the other tribal. In Africa, the former headquarters of colonial suppression and economic exploitation are seen as centers of "civilization." Thus, when persons from the rural areas enter the towns, they are labeled "detribalized," and are assumed to be free from the "tribal" ways of life. It will be shown that this kind of thinking is one of the ways in which Western scholarship justified the colonial system.

# THE CLASSICAL [EUROPEAN] WORLD AND AFRICA

Interest in the religion of African peoples dates back to the very dawn of Western scholarship. Some of the major issues in comparative religion, and the ethnocentricism—what in northern Uganda is expressed in the saying that "a child believes that his mother's cooking is the best in the world"—which has colored much of the reportage and interpretation of African cultures and religions can be traced to these early times.

The opinions of the classical scholars on African religions were dominated by Homer's poem. In the *Iliad* he wrote that the Greek deities were fond of visiting Ethiopia. Zeus, followed by all the gods, went to feast with the blameless Ethiopians, where he remained for twelve days. Poseidon also visited Ethiopia to receive a hecatomb of bulls and rams.

Herodotus of Halicarnassus, 484–428 BCE, presented a description of the religion of Egypt, and advanced hypotheses concerning its origin and its relation to the cults and mythologies of Greece.[27] The idea that some gods were kings or heroes who were deified, which is a central issue in the writings about divine kingship, has been propounded from the time of Herodotus.

In the same work Herodotus described the country and the inhabitants of the land to the east of Libya: "This is the tract of land in which the huge serpents are found and the lions, the elephants, the bears, the aspicts, and the horned asses, and the creatures without heads, whom the Libyans declare have their eyes in their breasts, *and also the wild men and the wild women.*"[28] Diodorus of Sicily restated the Homeric idea that Africans were just and pious: "And they say that they [Ethiopians] were the first to be taught to honor the gods and to hold sacrifices and festivals and processions and festivals and other rites by which men honor the deity; and that in consequence their piety has been published abroad among all men, and it is generally held that the sacrifices practiced among the Ethiopians are those that are the most pleasing to heaven."[29]

But elsewhere Diodorus described the Africans as follows, "The majority of them ... are black in color and have flat noses and woolly hair. As for their spirit, they are entirely savage and display the nature of wild beasts... and are far removed as possible from human kindness to one another; and speaking as they do with a shrill voice and cultivating none of the practices of civilized life as they are found among the rest of mankind, they are a striking contrast when considered in the light of our own."[30]

An African king called Piankhi [of ancient Nubia], 751–715 BCE, conquered Egypt; and the record of the conquest shows that the black ruler was scrupulously attentive to religious rituals, respectful of temples and the gods of Egypt. He refused to deal with conquered princes who were ceremoniously unclean, and was moderate in his relations with the vanquished. It would appear that it was from this episode that the idea of the piety of the African peoples became embedded in Greek mythology.[31]

Although the early Romans were well acquainted with Africans they did not furnish much information about African religions.[32] But Cicero, Julius Caesar and Tacitus wrote about the ancient Gauls and Germans whom they described as "Barbarians"; and Seneca restated the Stoic thesis that myths reveal either philosophical views on the basic nature of things or ethical doctrines. Much of present-day interpretation of myths is based on this thesis, and Evans-Pritchard's interpretation of Nuer deities as *refractions* of the Supreme

God, and Placide Tempels's supposed hierarchy of the "life force" of Bantu religion, may have their roots in the idea which arises from the same thesis, that the many divinities are aspects of one God.[33]

It is true that the Africans who entered the Greco-Roman world were neither romanticized nor scorned, and they were not subjected to racial discrimination.[34] But, despite the idea that Africans were pious and enjoyed the favor of the gods, the picture of African societies and peoples painted by the classical scholars is that of anarchy, promiscuity and cruel living. Some African peoples are even denied the possession of truly human form. They are described as strange and miserable folk who barely exist in continual hunger and fear. Catherine George has commented, "There was established thus early the pattern of thought which for many future centuries formed the basis for the approach to the 'primitives' of Africa, and which defined them not in terms of what they were and what they had, but in terms of what they presumably were not and had not, in terms, that is, of their inhumanity, their wildness and their lack of proper law."[35]

One of the most perplexing and amazing phenomena of Western scholarship is its almost morbid fascination and preoccupation with the "primitive," and the hostile and arrogant language of the philosophers, historians, theologians and anthropologists. Like the ogres of the tales of northern Uganda, unprovoked, Western scholars seek out peoples living in peace, and heap insults on their heads.

The role of Western scholarship in the colonial enterprise is discussed below. Here we note in passing that the glorious civilizations of Greece and Rome flourished on the institutions of slavery and imperialism. As Trevor-Roper put it, "It was Roman arms which conquered it; the Caesars who founded its institutions were Romans, and Rome was its capital. But in fact Rome was not its centre of gravity. The wealth which sustained it came largely from Asia and Africa. ... Africa supplied the City of Rome with two thirds of its corn. It was the conquest of Egypt which enabled Augustus to establish the Empire, the tribute of eastern provinces kept it going."[36] The democracy of Athens was a democracy among slave owners. The vast majority of the people had nothing to do or say about it.

Aristotle philosophized, "For that some rule and others are ruled is a thing not only necessary but expedient"; [and went on to say,] "From the hour of their birth, some are marked out for subjection, others for rule. ... It is clear then, that some men are by nature free, and others slaves, and that for the latter slavery is both expedient and right."[37] This division of the world's population into Greeks and barbarians, or free men by nature and slaves by nature, was not merely an "ego-flattering naïveté" in which Aristotle indulged.[38] It was an important myth justifying the institutions of slavery and imperialism. Indeed the authority of this hard-headed philosopher was invoked during the sixteenth century. The Spaniards did not hesitate to apply his doctrine of natural slavery to the [indigenous peoples of North America].[39] The Australian aborigines were decimated by the white settlers because "they were not regarded as human beings who had any rights at all."[40]

We [will] return to the myth of the "wild men" and "savages" [later]. But it is important to note that, even today, Western scholarship has not completely abandoned its traditional view of Africa. The world is still divided into the "civilized" West and the "primitive" non-Western world, now politely referred to as "The Developing Countries." For Trevor-Roper, for example, the study of African history is merely an amusement "with unrewarding gyrations of barbarous tribes in picturesque but irrelevant corners of the globe; tribes whose chief function in history... is to show to the present an image of the past from which by history, it has escaped."[41] Claude Levi-Strauss described the peoples studied by anthropologists as "...those primitives whose modest tenacity still offers us the means of assigning to human facts true dimensions. Men and women who, as I speak, thousands of miles away from here on some savannah ravaged by bush fire, or in some forest under torrential rain, are returning to camp to share the meager pittance or to invoke their gods together, those Indians of the tropics and their counterparts throughout the world who have taught me their humble knowledge soon, alas, destined for extinction under the impact of illness and—for them more horrible—modes of life with which we have plagued them."[42]

For over two thousand years, from Herodotus and Diodorus to Trevor-Roper and Levi-Strauss, Western scholars have provided the most powerful ideology for Western dominance over the rest of mankind. By systematic and intensive use of dirty gossip they have justified and explained away the plunder, murder and suppression carried out by Western man.[43]

The attainment of political *uhuru* (i.e., freedom) by many African states during the 1950s has swept away the subject of study of many white Africanists; and the plain language which was once used habitually without question in the days of robust self-confidence is rapidly becoming diplomatically taboo. The American anthropologist Ashley Montagu has urged Western scholars to drop the term "primitive" as it is no longer an expedient fiction. [In her words,] "In the rapidly developing world in which we live, in which the underdeveloped regions of the world will witness their most spectacular advances in the area of human development, it is of the first order of importance that the so-called civilized peoples of the world understand and act upon this fact."

The hostility of Christianity against the so-called "pagans" developed during the first three hundred years of its life, when the followers of Joshua the Messiah (*alias* Jesus Christ) were subjected to bloody and cruel persecutions both at the hands of the Jews and the Romans.[44] Jesus Christ himself was executed during the Feast of the Passover of 33 CE.[45] Stephen was stoned to death in accordance with the command of Deuteronomy that any Israelite who enticed his people to go after the gods of the heathen should be "stoned with stones that he die."[46]

At first Rome appeared to regard and treat Christianity in the same tolerant way as other cults that existed in the empire. But as it grew and presented a threat and a challenge the policy changed radically. The cult of Christ with its motto "Christ is Lord" was incompatible with the cult of Caesar.[47] In 64 CE the Emperor Nero blamed the Christians for the fire that destroyed Rome in that year; and ordered an official persecution. Peter was crucified head down, and Paul was beheaded. Ignatus the Bishop of Antioch in Syria, Polycarp the Bishop of Smyrna, Pollinus the Bishop of Lyons and many other church leaders fell victim to the persecution.[48] Several emperors, especially Decius (246–251 CE) instituted terrible persecutions throughout the empire, because Christianity had become too strong to be dealt with by local authorities. And, as Dimont put it, "It was a miracle that the Christians survived their first three hundred years. ... No sooner had Christianity become a separate religion than it was looked upon with suspicion by the Romans who now branded the Christians as subversive and subjected them to relentless persecution. A good number of their members were eaten by lions in the Roman amphitheatres, which was the Roman cure for Christianity, initiated by Nero and continued for three more centuries."[49]

But the so-called "pagan" onslaught did not consist of the sword, the lions' teeth and the cross only. Non-Christian scholars also wielded the most deadly pens. Porphyrinus wrote fifteen books entitled *Against the Christians*, and Bithynia wrote the *Hierocles*. The most extensive, passionate and comprehensive attack was launched by the Platonic Celsus, around 177–180 CE.[50] Celsus asked, what was the point of God coming down to earth? Was it in order to find out what was going on among men? Did he not know already? If he did, why did he not correct men merely by his divine power? Celsus likened the Christians to a cluster of bats or ants coming out of a nest, or frogs holding council around a marsh, or worms assembling in some filthy corner, disagreeing with one another about which of them are the most sinful. Jesus is portrayed as the offspring of an adulterous union of a poor Jewish country woman who earned her living by spinning, and a Roman soldier named Panthera. The woman was turned out by the carpenter who was engaged to her. The poor Jesus hired himself out us a workman in Egypt, and there learned the art of magic, and, full of conceit because of those powers, and on account of them, gave himself the title "God." Jesus collected around him ten or eleven infamous men, the most wicked tax collectors and sailors, with whom he fled here and there, collecting a means of livelihood in a disgraceful and inappropriate way. The reality of the death and resurrection of Christ is challenged at length: "If these things had been decreed for him and if he was punished in obedience to his Father ... why then does he utter loud laments and wailings, and pray that he may avoid the fear of death, saying, 'O Father, if this cup would pass by me?' And when he supposedly rose from the dead, Christ chose to show himself only to one crazy prostitute. Why did he not appear before Pilate or the Jews?"

There is a striking similarity between some of the writings of some of these ancient non-Christian scholars and present day African scholars. To be sure the African scholars today do not attack Christianity in the manner of Celsus. Their works resemble rather that of Philostatus, 175–247 CE. In his book, *The Life of Apolonius of Tyana*, he presented the religions of the Egyptians, Indians and Greeks so as to show the ideals of piety and tolerance. Modern African scholars do not only claim that African deities are eternal, omnipresent, omnipotent, etc., they also treat African cultures with pride and sympathy.

One of the most fascinating historical contradictions is that most of the outstanding figures in the counter-attack on the so-called "pagans" of early Christendom were also Africans: Manicus Felix, Lactantius, Cyprian, Firmicius, Maternus, Tertullian and St. Augustine. Danquah, Busia and Idowu declare that in West Africa even a child knows of the omnipotence of the African God.[51] But, long ago, the "assimilated" St. Augustine proclaimed, "*Omnes deos gentium deamonia*!" ("All the gods of the gentiles are demons!").

In his book *De Donatum*, 246 CE, Cyprian, Bishop of Carthage, stressed the superiority of Christian morality over that of the "pagan" world.[52] Commenting on the theatre in the cities he wrote, "Adultery is learnt as it is seen, while evil with public authority panders to vices, the matron who perchance had gone forth to the spectacle chaste returned from the spectacle unchaste. Then, further, how great a collapse of morals, what a stimulus to base deeds, what a nourishing of vices, to be polluted with the gestures of the actors." But Cyprian Kihangirye, Bishop of Gulu in northern Uganda, praises the high moral principles of the Lango. On their nudity he writes, "As in the Garden of Eden they did not know they were naked, and were perhaps in consequence much less prurient minded than is the case among the clothed Lango today. Morality then was much better than it is today."[53] And on polygamy John Mbiti has commented, "If the philosophical or theological attitude towards marriage is that those are an aid towards the partial recapture of the lost immortality the more wives a man has the more children he is likely to have, and the more children the stronger the power of immortality in that family."[54]

Although some of them are priests the present-day African scholars are first and foremost nationalists. Their works are in defense of African culture against the vicious attacks of Western scholarship. With Caelcilius, the "pagan" in helix's *Octavius*, they declare, "...since all peoples are firmly convinced that there are immortal gods. ... I cannot think there is anyone so audacious and so swollen with impious pretensions to wisdom as to destroy or weaken so ancient, useful and salutary a religion. ... Is it not then deplorable that an attack should be made upon the gods by certain fellows ... belonging to a party whose case is so hopeless, prescribed and desperate?"[55] This precisely was the point that Jomo Kenyatta was making in 1938.[56]

In 313 CE the Emperor Constantine issued the edict of Milan which granted toleration to the Christians and gave them equal rights with members of other cults. A few years later he himself became a Christian. His successor Julian, 361–363 CE, made a futile attempt to restore the Roman religion. And it is said that his last words were, "Pale Galilean, thou hast conquered." The Emperor Theodosius I, 378–395 CE, declared the "pagan" worship illegal, and as the state had once sought to destroy Christianity, so now it launched a bitter campaign to suppress "paganism."[57]

In the three centuries from 300 to CE 600 CE, four sets of laws were passed containing discriminatory provisions against non-Christians: Jews, Samaritans, Manicheans and heretics. The Manicheans belonged to a mystic Oriental religion which was carried from Asia Minor (western Asia) to Europe by soldiers. It became so popular with the masses that it represented a threat to the young church.

In 325 CE a church council met at Nicaea and adopted the Nicean Creed. After that, all the Christians had to believe in its principles; all other opinions were banned and declared heretical. And whereas in the past Christians settled their differences by discussion and conciliation, they now resorted to the sword to enforce religious conformity. The historian Gibbon has estimated that Christians killed more of their own numbers in the first hundred years after coming to power than did the Romans during the previous centuries.

The laws of Constantine, 315 CE, withdrew the rights of equality which were granted by the Emperor Caracalla in 212 CE, and forbade intermarriage between non-Christian men and Christian women. The laws of Theodosius II, 439 CE, prohibited non-Christians from holding high positions in the government, and the laws of Justinian, 531 CE, prohibited non-Christians from appearing as witnesses against Christians.

The dual purpose of these laws were to protect the infant church against the competition of other religions, and to preserve key posts for co-religionists. But they also clearly reflect the hostility of Christianity towards all other religions. The anti-Semitism which has bedeviled the Western world until the present day, and the contempt with which Western scholarship has treated African religions, are both very deeply rooted in the core of Western civilization.

The victory of Christianity signified the decline of the ancient civilization of Rome with its religious tolerance. When Rome collapsed the Christian church succeeded and superseded it. And it was upon the foundation of the triumphant but intolerant Christian religion, which was most hostile to the so-called "pagan" religions that the world of the Middle Ages was slowly built.

# SUPERSTITIONS OF WESTERN MAN

It is useful to discuss some of the dominant superstitions of the Western world during the Middle Ages, because, as we shall see, some of these superstitions persisted as far as the nineteenth century, and played important roles in determining the relationships between the inhabitants of Africa (and other areas of the globe) and the invaders. The most amusing, as well as important, of these was the belief in the existence of a kind of ogre known as the *wild man*.

Imaginary creatures such as the medieval *wild man* occur almost throughout the long history of Western civilization. The hairy beast man Enkmdi in the Babylonian epic Gilgamesh is the earliest on record. The classical [European] world, as we have seen, peopled the interior of Africa with imaginary beasts, some of which had their eyes in their stomachs. St. Augustine had a whole chapter in the *City of God* on "whether the descendants of Adam or the sons of Noah produced monstrous races of men." Among the most recent specimens is Tarzan, the movie hero. The Devil, satyrs, fauns, the legendary inhabitants of the Golden Age and the noble savage of the Age of Enlightenment are other imaginary creations of Western man. The frightening, man-eating ogre, *obibi*, some of which have ten eyes, and the diminutive but ever victorious *Lagitin* in the tales of northern Uganda, are the African equivalents of these medieval figures.

In medieval literature and art, the *wild man* is a hairy fellow compounded of human and animal traits. He is frequently shown wielding a heavy club or the trunk of a tree. His shaggy body is usually naked except for the twisted foliage worn around the loins. Was he a human being? Some medieval authorities answered this question in the affirmative. Heinrich von Hester, for instance, stated that the *wild men* were "Adam's children in form, face, and human intelligence, and are God's own handwork."[58] Others denied any connection between the *wild man* and human beings. How did he come to be in his lowly estate? Medieval thinkers held that it was the upbringing of the *wild man* among the wild beasts and the outrageous hardships that were responsible for his reduced state.

What were the social and psychological functions of such a belief? Bernheimer has suggested that the notion of the *wild man* was a response to a persistent psychological urge: the need to give external expression and symbolically valid form to the impulses of reckless physical self-assertion which are hidden in all of us, but are normally kept under control. [In short,] "His presence is like a running commentary with which a man's halfconscious imagery accompanies his conscious ideals and aspirations, a reminder that there are basic and primitive impulses clamoring for satisfaction."[59]

This may be the correct interpretation of the social and psychological functions of the belief in the *wild man*. It does not answer the question why Western man actually believed in its real existence. Spanish captains who went to fight in Mexico and Peru expected to encounter many of the mythical beings and monsters depicted in medieval literature: giants, pygmies, dragons, griffins, white haired boys, human beings with tails, headless creatures and other fabulous folk. Governor Valazque instructed Cortez to look out for strange beings with flat ears and others with dog-like faces whom he might encounter in Aztec lands. The Devil himself was to be found on certain islands of the Caribbean Sea. Francisco de Orella reported that he met the warrior women called the

Amazon during his famous voyage of 1540.⁶⁰ Most of these fictitious figures were later to appear in Africa.⁶¹

In northern Uganda little children probably believe that the *obibi* with ten eyes actually eats disobedient children, but adults know that this is only an imaginary *persona dramatis* of the tales. Why did civilized Europeans believe in the existence of human beings with tails and creatures without heads?

The period of early colonial expansion was the period of the Merchant Adventurers, of free looting and plundering expeditions, of the slave trade, of the conquest of newly discovered overseas territories, the extermination of the original inhabitants and establishment of colonial settlement by migration.⁶² From the belief in the imaginary creatures to identifying these creatures with the so-called Aborigines, was a very small step. Frobisher wrote that the American Indians "pluck and eat grass like brute beasts devouring the same" and "live in caves of the Earth, and hunt for their dinners or praye, even as the beare or other wild beasts do."⁶³ William den Rhyle described the [Khoisan] as lawless barbarians and immoral pagans who practiced only those habits to which blind impulse of nature irresistibly impels them. And another writer purporting to justify the Portuguese slave trade wrote of the Africans in bondage, "And so their lot was quite contrary to what it had been; since before they had lived in the perdition of the soul and body, of their soul, in that they were yet pagans, without the clearness of the light of the holy faith ... and worse than all, through the great ignorance that was in them, in that they had no understanding of good, but only knew how to live in bestial sloth."⁶⁴

The concept of the *wild man* provided for the white man a symbolism for the impulses of reckless self-assertion which are hidden in him, it also provided that *justification* for the unleashing of the same impulses of reckless self-assertion which found satisfaction in the wholesale massacre of the American Indians, Australian aborigines, the capture and enslavement of millions of Africans, etc.

During the eighteenth century men like Thunberg, Sparrman, Le Vaillant, Bruce, Mungo Park and others came to Africa primarily to explore and to observe. They had considerable background in the scientific and philosophical thought of the day. In their reports the earlier charges of bestiality and lawless promiscuity in African societies are absent, and African peoples are now presented as having religious beliefs, and even to have achieved some sort of a faith in a single deity.

This change of attitude which reflected a definite dissatisfaction with the inadequacies and injustices of Western civilization, has its roots in a major European intellectual tradition of "primitivism"— the belief that other, simpler societies were happier than their own. Believers in this tradition searched for and found what they called the *noble savage*: Africans, [indigenous peoples of the Americas], Australian aborigines etc., provided these creatures.

The object of this primitivistic critique was to make Western man live up to his supposed "civilized nature." The non-European was taken to be "civilized" because he was uncorrupted by civilization. The real purpose was not to assert the superiority of the [indigenous] American or African way of life over the European way of life. Those who spoke of the *noble savage* only wished to point out certain specific abuses, certain social inequalities and political tyrannies which they thought had intruded into civilized society, and were interfering with its growth. And, as Pearce put it, "Patently, it was a game, a case of old Ben Franklin, fur cap and all, speaking as he knew his French ladies would have him speak, and suggesting that, after till, things with high society are perhaps not quite so fine as they might seem."[65]

The idea of the *noble savage*, like that of the *wild man*, was a conceptual tool that Western scholars used in their analysis and criticisms of Western society. And although African societies were identified with the *noble savage*, social institutions of African peoples were not thereby better understood, because the Western scholars were not primarily interested in African social institutions.

# PRESENT STUDIES IN AFRICAN RELIGIONS [CA. 1970]

Present day studies of African religions may be divided into three related categories:
(a) The Christian apologists mounting a counter-attack on the eighteenth and twentieth centuries' non-believers.
(b) African nationalists fighting a defensive battle against the vicious onslaught on African cultures by Western scholarship; and
(c) The missionaries scheming what they call "a dialogue with animism."

All three groups are reactions, and are heavily influenced, limited and controlled by the forces against which they react. The Christian apologists like Evans-Pritchard, Godfrey Lienhardt and Geoffrey Parrinder address their works mainly to Western scholars and churchmen. They use African deities to prove that the Christian God does exist, and is known also among African peoples. The African nationalists like Jomo Kenyatta, Leopold Sedar Senghor, J. B. Danquah, K. A. Busia and John Mbiti protest vigorously against any Western scholar who describes African cultures and religions in disparaging terms. Their works are mainly addressed to the *unbelieving* Europeans, and they attempt to show that the African peoples were as civilized as the Western peoples. They dress up African deities with Hellenic robes and parade them before the Western world. The missionaries like Edwin Smith, John Taylor and Placide Tempels have for their audience the highly sensitive and easily provoked new African elites, whose hearts they wish to win for the Christian God. They attempt to assure the Africans that the earlier generations of anthropologists erred grievously when they reported that African peoples were mere "pagan savages," and assert that Africans are, as they have always been, highly religious and moral peoples.

The eighteenth century philosophers and the nineteenth century anthropologists used African and other non-Western religions to demonstrate their theories of "progress," which is but another version of the myth of the "primitive." In 1757 the Scottish philosopher David Hume wrote *The Natural History of Religion* in which he argued, "If we consider the improvement of human society from rude beginnings to the state of greater perfection, polytheism or idolatry, was, and necessarily must have been, the first and most ancient religion of mankind." In his 1764 book *Emile*, Jean Jacques Rousseau argued along the same line: "Laban's grotesques, savage manitous, Negro fetishes, all the works of man and nature, were the first deities of mortals. Polytheism was their first religion and idolatry their cult."

Voltaire published his *Dictionnaire Philosophie* in 1766 and there he proposed that men began by knowing a single God, and that it was later that human weakness adopted a number of deities. Surprisingly, this was identical to the official Christian doctrine that man is by nature religious, and that the belief in one God was revealed by God himself to Adam, while polytheism was a diabolical counterfeit. This has led Pettazzoni to remark, "Voltaire, the unbeliever, the rationalist, the pitiless mocker, was thus in agreement for once, on an important point with the doctrine of the Church."[66] However, in his *Philosophy of History* published in 1766, Voltaire expanded on the subject of religion of the first man. He wrote, "Volumes might have been written upon this subject; but all these volumes might be reduced to two words, which are that the majority of mankind were for a long time in a state of imbecility, and that, perhaps the most imbecile of all were those who wanted to discover a signification in these absurd fables, and ingrained reason upon folly."

If David Hume and Rousseau were the high priests of the superiority of Western culture in that they placed Christianity at the top of the ladder of "progress," and what they supposed were the religions of other peoples at the bottom, Voltaire's interest in the supposed religion of the first men was to arm himself for an attack on Christianity itself. This he did by first equating Christianity with the supposed beliefs of the earliest human society, and labeling them all "insensibility and imbecility."

In the nineteenth century Auguste Comte, the positivist philosopher, sketched a picture of development of the human mind through three stages:

(a) The religious, from the beginning to the fourteenth century,
(b) The metaphysical, from the fourteenth to the eighteenth century, and
(c) The positive, the nineteenth century.

The religious stage again subdivides into three periods: Fetishism, Polytheism and Monotheism. The supposed religion of African peoples, that is fetishism, thus comes at the bottom of the ladder.

Edward Burnett Tylor, the English anthropologist, took up Comte's scheme, but with "animism" as the oldest form of religion. Frazer set forth his paradigm of phases of thought through which all peoples pass in *The Golden Bough* (1890). According to this, man first believed in magic, then in religion and finally he became scientific.

We need not go into a critique of the idea of "progress," which, as I have stated above, is only the other side of the coin of the myth of the "primitive." Nor is it necessary to discuss at any length, the concepts of "fetishism" or "animism" because these were not African religions, but what the eighteenth century philosophers and the nineteenth century anthropologists supposed were African concepts. The missionaries planning a "dialogue between Christianity and animism" waste their time, because there is no such religion as animism in Africa. But we can be sure that these Western scholars were engaged in perpetuating the myth of the superiority of the Western culture over those of African peoples now under colonial domination. And it is to this arrogance with which African deities were treated that African scholars today react.

Moreover, even after the rejection of the evolutionistic theories of the nineteenth century, leading Western anthropologists continue to use the insulting terms when describing African institutions. In her book *Primitive Government*, Lucy Mair defends her position as follows: "It is a fact of history that it was the European peoples who discovered these others, and in most cases established dominion over them, and not vice versa.... The European peoples had ships and methods of navigation which enabled them to travel further, *and weapons which generally enabled them to win any battles in which they were involved....* In all these fields the techniques of the peoples who came under European rule were rudimentary, and in consequence their systems of government might also be called rudimentary. This is one sense of the word 'primitive'; and it is the only sense in which a modern anthropologist would use the word."[67]

In 378 Roman armies were defeated by Germanic invaders in the battle of Adrianople. In 410 Rome itself was sacked and occupied by Alaric, king of the Goths. In 476 Romulus

Augustulus, the last Roman emperor in the West, lost his throne and soon the invaders gained full control of the western half of the Roman Empire. Jerome lamented the fall of Rome in the following words, "The world sinks into ruin.... The renowned city, the capital of the Roman Empire, is swallowed up in one tremendous fire; and there is no part of the earth where Romans are not in exile."[68] But Western scholarship insists that the victorious Goths, Sarmatians, Alans, Huns, Vandals and Marchmen who brought proud Rome to her knees were "Barbarians." But the European barbarians who ravaged Africa and the entire globe are called "Civilizers."

Evans-Pritchard pleaded, "But the words are used by me in... a value-free sense, and they are etymologically unobjective. In any case, the use of the word 'primitive' to describe persons living in small-scale societies with simple material culture and lacking literature is too firmly established to be eliminated."[69] In North America, Australia and Melanesia anthropologists studied remnants of defeated and demoralized Aborigines, mostly living on reservations. In Africa they encountered vigorous societies with characteristics which distinguished them from the classical "simple societies" of the anthropologists. Meyer Fortes wrote, "One of these is the relatively great size, in terms of both the territorial spread and of numbers, of many ethnographic units in Africa. There are few truly isolated societies in Africa. Communication takes place over wide geographical regions, and movements of groups over long stretches of time, exactly like those that are known from our own history, have spread languages, beliefs, customs, craft, food producing techniques, and the network of trade and government over large areas with big populations."[70]

If these highly emotive terms are etymologically unobjectionable to the Welshman, they have hurt Africans a great deal, and African scholars have reacted strongly in a number of ways.[71] Some have sought to demonstrate that Africa has a past as glorious as that of other nations or peoples. [Cheikh] Anta Diop, for example, has claimed that the early Egyptian civilization was essentially a Negro one; and that, therefore, all Africans can draw the same moral advantage from it that Westerners draw from the Greco-Roman civilization.[72] Leopold Sedar Senghor, the chief proponent of *negritude*, has attempted to distinguish between the African and the European in terms of intellect and sensibility. [Senghor claimed,] "Emotion is black... reason Greek," and then [began] to sing praises to black sensibility.[73]

In the field of religious studies African students have responded with a vigorous condemnation and rejection of the claims of Western scholarship which presented their peoples as "primitive pagans." But, instead of carrying out systematic studies of the beliefs of their peoples, and presenting them as the African peoples actually know them, the African scholars, smarting under the insults from the West, claimed that African peoples knew the Christian God long before the missionaries told them about it. African deities were selected and robed with awkward Hellenic garments by Jomo Kenyatta, J. B. Danquah, K. A. Busia, W. Abraham, E. B. Idowu and others.

In 1962 Geoffrey Parrinder warned that African nationalist scholars must not glorify the past so much that they come to believe that African religion might naturally have developed by itself to the heights of Christianity. In 1969 and 1970 John Mbiti published his two volumes in which, in the style of the *Golden Bough*, he gathered the works of every known scholar, including Parrinder himself, who ever helped to select, Hellenize and Christianize an African deity.[74] But while the purpose of Frazer's monumental work was to discredit Christianity by showing how one of its essential features, the resurrection of Jesus Christ, is analogous to what is found in "pagan" religions, Mbiti's books are intended to show to the world not only that "African peoples are not religiously illiterate," but also that the African deities are but local names of the One God who is omniscient, omnipresent, omnipotent, transcendent and eternal.[75]

But there was another reason why the nineteenth century anthropologists were greatly interested in African and other non-Christian religions. As Evans-Pritchard has noted, the scholars whose writings have been most influential, men like Tylor, Krazer, Marret, Malinowski, Durkheim and Freud were agnostics or atheists. What then had they to do with African religions? "They sought and found in primitive religions a weapon which could, they thought, be used with deadly effect against Christianity. If primitive religion could be explained away as an intellectual aberration, as a mirage induced by emotional stress, or by its social function, it was implied that the higher religions could be discredited and exposed in the same way."[76]

In *The Future of an Illusion*, Sigmund Freud pleaded that man cannot remain a child forever; he must venture into the hostile world.[77] Elsewhere he wrote that to the ordinary man religion was a system of doctrines and pledges that explained the riddle of the world and assured him that a solicitous Providence was watching over him. "The whole thing is so patently infantile, so incongruous with reality," declared Karl Marx.[78] "The abolition of religion as the illusory happiness of the people is required for their real happiness."[79] "Every man who occupies himself with the construction of a God," Lenin wrote, "or merely even agrees to it, prostitutes himself in the worst way, for he occupies himself with self-contemplation and self-reflection, and tries thereby to deify his most unclean, most stupid, and most servile features or pettiness."[80] And Frazer, writing on the execution of Christ stated, "In the great army of martyrs who in many lands, not only in Asia, have died a cruel death in the characters of Gods, the devout Christian will doubtless discern types and forerunners of the Coming Savior— stars that herald in the morning sky the advent of the Son of Righteousness. ... The skeptic, on the other hand, with equal confidence, will reduce Jesus of Nazareth to the level of a multitude of other victims of barbarous superstition, and will see in him no more than a moral teacher."[81]

These and many other latter day "pagans," who, in the same vein as their earlier clansmen (e.g., Celsus, Porphyrinus and Voltaire), attack, mock and challenge the Christian faith, have provoked modern day "apologists" into action. And they have all reacted along predictable lines: by restating the official Christian doctrine that man is naturally religious, and then using African deities to show that God was known even among African peoples.

Evans-Pritchard's The Aquinas Lecture of 1959 entitled "Religion and the Anthropologists" and his book *Theories of Primitive Religion* are a determined counter-attack on these later day "pagans." In his "Zande Theology" and *Nuer Religion* he boldly interpreted the *Mbori* of Zande religion and the *Kwoth* of the Nuer in terms of the Christian God. Other modern day "apologies" are Godfrey Leinhardt's article "Religion" in *Man, Culture and Society*; *African Traditional Religion* by Geoffrey Parrinder and Lienhardt's *Divinity and Experience* are other attempts to interpret African deities in terms of the Christian God.

The important contributions of these outstanding scholars is that they brushed away the cobwebs that cluttered much of the nineteenth century speculative writings on African religions by carrying out systematic research using the languages of the peoples they studied. One's quarrel with them is on their interpretation of the material. It is understandable that they should have done this in terms of the Christian God, because it was the existence of this God and their religion that they set out to defend. Evans-Pritchard protested, "Why therefore should those who held, and hold, that religion is just one social institution among others and that all institutions are just as much natural systems or part of them, as organisms and celestial bodies, feel called upon to undermine it?" And quoting Benjamin Kidd with approval, he continued, "If social scientists were to enquire unemotionally into the social function of a phenomenon so universal and so persistent they would discover that the vitality of societies, even their existence, is bound up with religion, and that it is precisely through religious systems that social evolution, or progress, has been brought about, for it is the most significant of evolutionary forces, the chief agent in natural selection."[82]

It may be true that the vitality of African societies is bound up with their religious beliefs and practices. It is therefore highly important that these beliefs be properly understood. The interpretation of African deities in terms of the Christian God does not help us to understand the nature of the African deities as African peoples conceive them. As Godfrey Lienhardt admitted, "The attributes of our God and their (Dinka) Nhialic are not identical.... To use the word God would raise metaphysical and semantic problems of our own for which there is no parallel among the Dinka."[83]

# Dialogue with Animism

The works of missionaries on African religions reflect the vital interests of the Christian churches to know the nature of the beliefs of other peoples, with the ultimate aim of converting them. Recently the Catholic church estimated that there were two billion human beings in the world today who live "in the power of darkness and of Satan" because they have not yet heard the gospel message, and their number was growing daily. It is stated that Africa, Asia and Oceania were the areas where the vast majority of populations had not yet been markedly affected by the gospel.[84]

The mission of the church, according to Giovanni Battista Montini, consists in extending Christ's life throughout the world and in helping mankind to participate in his mysteries. In order to achieve this the church adapts itself to the thoughts, culture, customs and languages of different ages and peoples.[85] As early as 1244 Pope Innocent sent four priests to study the religion and customs of the Mongols. One of these, Jean du Plau Carpin, wrote a book entitled *The History of the Mongols*. In 1553, William Ruysbroek was sent by Pope Louis IX to do research among the Manichaeans and Saracens. The writings of these early Vatican "anthropologists" provided material for scholars such as the Franciscan Schoolman, Roger Bacon.[86] Modern anthropological and linguistic studies by missionaries include works by Koscoe, Willoughby, Boccassine, Tarantino and Crazzolara.

Although the oldest Christian church in Africa, the Ethiopian Orthodox Church, was established in the fourth century, it has not exerted any direct influence on, or taken an active part in, any extension of the Christian faith to the rest of Africa. The Christian missionaries came to Africa from Europe and later from North America. By 1500, the Portuguese missionaries preached at the courts of the kingdoms of Benin and Congo. It is reported that a son of a Congolese chief became a priest, and after studies in Portugal was crowned a bishop in 1518. By the mid-seventeenth century the Jesuits had established a monastery in São Paulo de Luanda in the Congo. Other Jesuits pushed their way inland from the mouth of the Zambezi into present day Zimbabwe. By 1652, a paramount chief was converted and baptized.[87]

By the end of the eighteenth century, however, all these missions had disintegrated almost completely. A new missionary movement to Africa began about this time, initiated by the Protestant churches, as a direct result of the evangelical revival in Europe. The new movement was closely connected with the elements in Britain which were engaged in fighting against the slave trade.

The Christian mission to Africa was double-edged. The missionaries came to preach the gospel as well as to "civilize," and in their role of "civilizers" they were at one with the colonizing forces; indeed they were an important vehicle of Western imperialism, which readily lent to the churches its wealth, power and influence. As Beetham put it, "With the partition of Africa following the Berlin conference European rule began to provide an umbrella of law and order for missionary activity. A settled government, the telegraph, the railway—all helped."[88]

The missionaries came with the same arrogant assumptions that they represented a "higher" civilization, indeed, perhaps that no civilization existed in Africa. Western values and customs were, to them, identical with Christian morality. "They insisted on even minor observances as necessary outward and visible signs of an inward 'civilized' state." One missionary, on the occasion of his first wedding anniversary at Badagri (Gbagle) in Nigeria, gave a tea party which he described as a token of civilization.[89]

The language of the eighteenth and nineteenth century missionaries was exactly the same as that of the colonialists. In 1710 Father Cipriano described the Warri in Nigeria as "obstinate, idolatrous and given to witchcraft and all sorts of abominable vices."[90] Bishop Tucker dubbed the religion of the Baganda "the Lubare superstition," and called its priests "Doctors of Satanity." In his opinion the Baganda "truly suffered through the long ages of darkness and gloom as a result of cruelties and bloodshed connected with this faith."[91] In 1851 a black American bishop was sent to Sierra Leone. Anna Scott described his progress in her book, *Day Dawn in Africa*. She talked about the gross spiritual darkness which enveloped the heathen, and called the deity of the Grebos "The Grand Devil," and its priest "demon doctor."[92]

In 1937, Dietrich Westermann urged missionaries to be ruthless with African religions. The missionary might be anxious to appreciate and to retain indigenous social and moral values, but in the case of religion he had to be ruthless, because the religion that he taught was opposed to the existing one, and one had to cede to the other.[93] This was the confident language of bygone time, of the time when Western imperialism in all its forms, including the missionary, still looked upon the whole of Africa as its own backyard in which it could do exactly as it pleased. But things began to change rapidly when the nationalist forces in Africa began to challenge these assumptions. As Warren put it, "We are called upon to recognize that in the world of our time there is widespread revolt against any form of domination by the West." The Christian church now sees itself in direct confrontation with African religions. "No longer content to be on the defensive, they are now offering themselves as answers to the questionings of mankind."[94]

The changed situation has forced the missionaries to review and change their tactics. There is, for example, the attempt to extricate Christianity from its past historical association with Western political, economic and cultural aggression. "The Cross, after all," Warren pleaded, "was not a symbol of imperial domination but of the *imperium* of sacrifice." And in the place of arrogance, the Christian is asked to have "a deep humility." [Warren continued,] "Our first task in approaching another people, another culture, another religion is to take off our shoes, for the place we are approaching is holy. Else we may find ourselves treading on men's dreams."[95]

This is the basis of the so-called "Dialogue with Animism," a profound conversation envisaged between the Christian and the "pagan" mind, in which the former does not talk down as if to a child. Beetham has estimated that of the 230 million people south of the Sahara, 55 million are Muslims, 60 million Christians and the rest, 115 million, Animists.[96] According to Louis-Vincent Thomas, "animism" is a metaphysico-religious conception which introduces a multiplicity of intermediate beings between God and man.[97]

We note that this definition of "animism" differs greatly from Tylor's original idea. Tylor sought to explain the origin of religion and how it developed. But he also regarded spiritual beings as illusions, the product of immature or primitive minds. The definition of "animism" above, derives from Placide Tempels's speculations of Bantu philosophy, and is based on a belief in God.[98] It is a crude marriage between what Tylor supposed was the religion of the earliest man and what later anthropologists and missionaries conjectured, namely that African peoples believe in a High God. Neither case represents a true picture, since they are not results of detailed and objective studies, but speculations by interested "apologists." "Animism," "Fetishism" or belief in a High God are products of the Western mind. There are no "animists" in Africa.

# Max Muller, the Missionaries and African Deities

Evans-Pritchard wrote, "The word for ghost, *joagh*, is found in various forms in all the Nilotic languages. In most of the Shulluk-Luo group of languages it means 'God' or 'Spirit.' In some of the Nilotic languages, including Nuer, the word is either the same as, or is closely related to, that used to denote plagues, pestilences, murrains and indeed any serious sickness; and that being so, it is perhaps wise to point out that such calamities are not thought to come from ghosts but from God."[99] In his book, *Concepts of God in Africa*, John Mbiti collected the deities of some three hundred African peoples, all of which were called God.

It was Max F. Muller, who first identified the Christian God with "pagan" deities! Early European travelers reported that African peoples, in common with other so-called "savages," had no religion, but only superstitions. The nineteenth century anthropologists represented Africans as being totally immersed in religion, but having no conception of a High God. Following Max Muller, some missionaries and anthropologists began to refer to African deities as God.

We note, to begin with, that this was contrary to Christian teaching. The Christian faith seems to contain a certain amount of atheism with regard to certain deities which it cannot tolerate. Charges of atheism were leveled at early Christians, and these were readily admitted. Justin, for example, is reported to have said, "We are called atheists. And yes, we confess it, we are atheists to those so-called gods."[100] The Catholic theologian, Jacques Muritain, has written, "With regard to those gods, the saint is a perfect atheist."[101] Furthermore, us we have seen, while not denying the existence of "pagan" deities, St. Augustine held that they were devils. Why then were "pagan" deities identified with the Christian God? How did *jok* come to be called God?

One great dilemma which the missionaries faced was what name they should call their God when they preached to African peoples. Some of them held that "pagan" terms could never express the Christian truth adequately. Among the northern Nilotes, Catholic priests introduced the Italian word, *Dio*; and among the Alur, Protestant priests used the Kiswahili term, *Mungu*. In Acoli-land *jok* was first used by the Protestants, and then *Allah*, but later this was again dropped in preference to *rubanga*. Wright reported, "It was the then head of the Mission who abolished *jok* in favor of *rubanga*. He had formerly been among the Two tribe in the Sudan, where he encouraged the abolition of *jok* in favor of the Italian *Dio* (!) His chief professed reason was that it was very inconvenient that *jok* should be used for 'God' as that word made part of the word *la-jok* meaning black magician; besides, he would say, *jok* was not the same as 'God,' as very ignoble things would occasionally be said of *jok*."[102] Other missionaries were concerned that Africans might come to regard Christianity as a white man's religion. It was therefore of paramount importance that Christianity should be preached as the full expression of what Africans had been groping for. As Willoughby put it in 1928, "We must take pains to preach the truth to the African that he may not take it for something foreign to his own, which means that we must link it with the best of his aspirations."[103]

Closely related to this latter attitude was the strong assumption that a belief in a High God was universal. Max Muller himself held that from the very dawn of history and from the first dawn of our individual conscience, man has always been face to face with the Infinite.[104] Edwin Smith, Parrinder and John Taylor found it impossible to dispute a universal recognition and a desire for the Ultimate God.[105] "I assume in this book," John Mbiti wrote in 1970, "that there is but One Supreme God. I take it also that the majority of the concepts presented here, have sprung independently out of African reflection on God."[106]

It is now known, however, that the conception of a Supreme Being is not universal. The central truth of Threvada Buddhism is the *nirvana*, the abode of peace beyond the round of re-births, but not about a personal God. In Hinduism there are two levels of truth: truth about the Absolute, and truth about the world, and the latter has only a provisional and secondary significance. Belief in a personal creator belongs to the second level, because the creator of an illusory world shares its illusoriness. Ninian Smart has summed up the issue aptly, "For how often do we read ... that some kind of a belief in God is to be found in all cultures? And haven't we comforted ourselves in days of doubt that the great majority of men have believed in some sense, in God? Can this almost universal testimony be utterly without foundation? Such is the way we have been brought up to think. But wrongly."[107]

However, the missionaries proceeded to look for what they believed were the local names of the Supreme God. They studied riddles, proverbs, folk tales, myths and songs, and listened to ordinary conversation, in the hope that the name of God might be discovered, or they asked leading questions such as "who created you?" Because of the widespread use of these dubious methods of studying a people's religion, and especially among African scholars, we should pause to examine them briefly.[108]

In 1911, Italian Catholic priests put before a group of Acoli elders the question "Who created you?"; and because the Luo language does not have an independent concept of *create* or *creation*, the question was rendered to mean, "Who molded you?" But this was still meaningless, because human beings are born of their mothers. The elders told the visitors that they did not know. But, we are told that this reply was unsatisfactory, and the missionaries insisted that a satisfactory answer must be given. One of the elders remembered that, although a person may be born normally, when he is afflicted with tuberculosis of the spine, then he loses his normal figure, he gets "molded." So he said, "*Rubanga* is the one who moulds people." This is the name of the hostile spirit which the Acoli believe causes the hunch or hump on the back. And, instead of exorcising these hostile spirits and sending them among pigs, the representatives of Jesus Christ began to preach that *rubanga* was the Holy Father who created the Acoli.[109] Whenever we read that an African people believed in a "creator," we can be assured that it is the result of such soliciting on behalf of the reporter. African religions are not so much concerned about the *beginning* and the *end* of the world, they are rather more concerned with the good life here and now, with health and prosperity, with success in life, happy and productive marriage, etc.; they deal with the causes of diseases, with failures and other obstacles in the path of self-realization and fulfillment.

This leads directly to the consideration of the so-called "myths of origin" in African religions. Perhaps because Christianity has a myth of origin, missionaries and other students of African religions felt it necessary to seek African equivalents of the story of the Garden of Eden. The first thing to note is that the stories that have been collected and labeled "Myths of origin" have no religious significance. They do not form any part of religious activity; and although a few of them may be described as poetic discussions of how things came to be as they are, the vast majority of them are ordinary moral tales. The most well known of these is the story of two messengers, the *Chameleon* and the *Weaver bird*.[110] The moral of the story is clear, namely that slowness can bring death. Nobody, except perhaps the missionaries and some other students of African religions, believes that this was how death came into the world, in the same way that the Jews and Christians believe (or used to believe) in the Genesis story of creation.

And how could anybody learn about a people's religion by studying their riddles? In northern Uganda this is a game of words in which mostly children and young people indulge. It is simply a matter of remembering the right set of questions or problems and the right set of answers or solutions. For example, the answer to the problem, "Two doves fly across the stream," is "Eyes." Any other answer like "Ears," "Legs," which could be equally *correct*, are not acceptable.

Of all the areas of people's cultural activity, the riddle is perhaps the most barren of religious material. The other equally barren area is the "proverb," in that most of these pithy sentences are social commentaries and teachings. The oft-quoted one from West Africa that "No one teaches a child God," does not mean that West African children are born with the knowledge of "God," because, in fact, children do not know about deities until they are taught about them.[111] This proverb means that certain things are so obvious that even a little child ought to know about them. It is a commentary on the stupidity or ignorance of some adult.

It is accepted that songs and chants sung at religious ceremonies are a useful source of information, but other songs, such as beer party songs, love songs and war songs have little to contribute to the religion of a people.

The missionaries did not carry out systematic studies in order to determine, first of all, whether or not Africans believed in a High God, and, secondly, if they did, what His/Its/Her name was. They were so completely convinced of the universality of the belief in a High God, that they thought all that was needed was to discover the name.

Now, although he identified "pagan" deities with the Christian God, Max Muller described the "pagan" deities as "imperfect" and even "childish." [He wrote,] "However imperfect and however childish the concept of God may be, it always represents the highest ideal of perfection which the human soul for the time being can reach."[112] The missionaries proceeded to remove the supposed "imperfection" and "childishness" by teaching and preaching. John Taylor commented, "The Gospel adds dimensions to the image of the transcendent which the wit of man could never have devised."[113] Edwin Smith quoted the English rendering of a hymn composed by Unsikana, one of the first Xhosa converts, in which the Xhosa deity called *uThixo* was identified with Jesus Christ. Part of the hymn goes as follows:

> It is thou (uThixo) who sittest in the highest
> Thou art the creator of life
> The creator who madest heaven also
> The shooting stars declare it to us
> Thou art he whose hands are with wounds
> Thou art he whose feet are with wounds
> Thou art he whose blood was spilled for us....

Was this Xhosa deity ever crucified on the cross so as to sustain wounds on its hands and feet? Did some Roman soldiers stab it with a lance in the chest? But Edwin Smith commented, "This is what *uThixo* had come to mean to a Xhosa of the first generation. Perhaps the original etymological sense of the word matters little, after all."[114] But, of course, the original etymological sense of the word matters a great deal to someone who is primarily interested in the conception of gods as Africans see them, rather than in the *Christianized* conceptions of these deities, the result of many years of preaching and teaching.

If the missionaries called African deities God because they believed that these were the local names of the Supreme God, and also because they sought to meet the Africans on their own ground, Western anthropologists were confronted with a different problem: that of interpreting African deities and religious ideas to the Western world. This they could only do in terms of Western concepts. The anthropologists to whom the soul and gods had no reality interpreted African religions in terms of psychological, biological or sociological theories. Christian anthropologists, on the other hand, described African religious beliefs in Christian concepts, and called African deities God.[115]

As Lienhardt has written, "In deriving religion ultimately from a God we believe in, or from psychological needs, or from society itself, we are substituting for the tribesman's beliefs something we can take for granted—whether our God, or psychology or society. Each general theory is thus, a way, a substitute for any particular religion, an alternative way of giving account of these situations which different tribes give account of...."[116] And Evans-Pritchard confessed, "One can only interpret what one sees in terms of one's own experience, and of what one is.... The personality of the anthropologist cannot be eliminated from his work.... Fundamentally, in his account of a primitive people the anthropologist is not only describing their social life as accurately as he can, but is expressing himself also. In this sense his account must express moral judgment, especially where it touches matters on which he feels strongly: and what comes out of a study will, to this extent, at least, depend on what the individual brings to it."[117]

Like Max Muller, the Western anthropologists who interpreted African deities in terms of the Christian God, described them as "inadequate," "sometimes misleading," etc. We [will] return to the question of comparison of the Christian God and African deities [later]. Here we may mention the possibility of the influence of "public opinion" on these Western scholars. For, although the present-day anthropologists cannot be accused of any kind of fear or bias in their teaching and writings, it is wise to bear in mind that they are active members of their own churches and other institutions, and their first allegiance is to their God, whom they believe to be supreme. Max Muller was caught up in the evolutionistic theory, and he saw "pagan" religions as stages of evolution. "Pagan" deities could not, therefore, be of the same "development" as the God of Christendom. But, even then, we are told, "The famous Max Muller... trod warily—the Bishop of Gloucester had already condemned attempts 'to put into competition sacred books of India and the Holy Scriptures.'"[118] Max Muller was not elected to the Chair of Sanskrit at Oxford in 1860, partly because he was a German, but it was also said his teaching was subversive to the Christian faith. Another example is that of Levy-Bruhl who privately held that Christianity and Judaism were superstitions, but dared not make any allusions to them "in order not to cause offence."[119]

As we have noted above, African scholars, trying to interpret the religious ideas of their countrymen in terms of European thought, and also anxious to defend Africa from the intellectual arrogance of the West, presented African deities complete with the attributes of the Christian God. Busia asserted that to most Ashanti people the world was ruled from afar by a Supreme Being who was all-wise, all-powerful, etc., the creator of all things. Danquah, Kenyatta, Idowu and Mbiti wrote along the same line; and William Abraham thought that there was an Akan *theology* involving a Supreme Being who was omnipotent, omnipresent, omniscient, etc.

It is interesting to note that the African scholars have not described the deities of their people as "imperfect," "childish" or "inadequate." I think this was not because they were convinced that there were no competent methods by which deities of different peoples could be measured or weighed and otherwise compared, but because they were combating these very disparaging assertions of Western scholars about African religious conceptions.

## WHAT THEN IS JOK?

*Etymological Answer*

Like the Anglo-Saxon word *god*, *jok* of the Nilotes is a class word. The Nilotes do not speak of *jok* without adding the "proper name" or specifying clearly the category and also the particular *jok* they have in mind. When referring to a chiefdom *jok*, the name of chiefdom as well as the proper name of the particular *jok* is mentioned: for example, *jok baka me Patiko*, Jok Baka of Patiko; *jok lokka me Koc*, Jok Lokka of Koc; etc. When clansmen gather at the ancestral shrine, *abila*, the ancestors invoked are called by their names. The hostile spirits which cause diseases also have proper names: e.g., *jok odude*; *jok anyodo*; *jok kulu*; etc. The harmful "power" of the witch is called *jok*, and it is identified by reference to the name of the witch, e.g., *jok pa Lapyem*, Jok of Lapyem. And the *jok-in-the-bundle* which is brought from afar, bears the name of the country from which it comes, e.g., *jok loka*, Jok from Bunyoro; *jok madi*, Jok from Madi.[120]

When the Nilotes encounter *jok*, it is with a specific and named or easily definable *jok*, and not some vague "power" that they communicate with. The proper name identifies the *jok*, placing it in a specific category and social context, for action. There is no occasion when the Nilotes think of all the *jogi* (pl. of *jok*) simultaneously. And there is no evidence to show that they regard the named *jogi* as refractions, or manifestations, or hypostases of a so-called High God. Each category of *jok* is independent of other *jogi*, although some are used against others. For the Nilotes there are many deities. Not one.

*The "Things" Called Jok*

The Nilotes represent their deities in different forms, some material, others non-material: "soil" from the "original" homeland; a large rock, said to have fallen from the sky entombing dancers; snakes, some said to have human heads; men-like creatures which "fell" from the sky and broke their thighs; ghosts of ancestors; spirits in the head of the diviner, kites flying with flames in their anuses, and free spirits which can be captured and "killed." These images fulfill an essential purpose. They focus and enclose the particular *jok*, so that men can get their minds round it, and have something to fix their imagination, and also to direct their prayers, sacrifices or attacks.

This is another aspect of the tendency among the Nilotes to individualize and concretize the objects of their belief. Not only do the *jogi* have proper names, but they can also be, as it were, known through the senses. The "soil" from the supposed original homeland is handled and carried from place to place. The rock can be seen and touched; the kites with the flame in their anuses can be seen flying through the night sky; the voices of the ghosts of the dead ancestors can be heard and identified as belonging to so-and-so; the *jok-in-the-bundle* can be bought and sold, and it makes noises like chicks, and when buried in the ground the earth around cracks. The free hostile spirits can be heard arguing with the diviner, and when captured and killed, their blood can be seen on the blade of the weapon. This is in vivid contrast with the metaphysical aspects of Christianity with its conception of an eternal world revealed only to the intellect, but not to the senses. As John Robinson wrote, "In the pagan world it was, and still is a matter of mental images. For us [Christians] it is a question of mental images."[123]

*Jok as an Object of Ritual Action*

The Nilotes are concerned not with ontological definitions but with dynamic function. The *jogi* are objects of ritual activities which they believe promote the well-being of a group or of an individual, or combat actual or threatened ill-health or misfortune. Once a year the entire chiefdom was a mobilized around the chiefdom *jok*, and sacrifices and prayers were offered for the health and prosperity of the whole people.[122] Clansmen would gather at the ancestral shrine and invoke the ghosts of their ancestors to protect the living members of the clan. The hostile spirits which caused ill-health would be given some form of gift, and asked to leave the patient alone. If they accepted the gift, they would be escorted in a friendly way towards the place of their abode. But if they refused it they would be captured and killed. The role of the diviner was to identify the particular *jok* responsible for ill health or ill luck; the group concerned would hire the diviner and act according to his prescriptions.

*Jok as a Means of Interpreting Ill Health or Misfortune*

The Nilotes interpret most of their misfortunes in terms of *jok*. Misfortunes that befall or threaten to affect the entire chiefdom, are attributed to the chiefdom *jok*. The ghosts of the ancestors visit the living with illness if they are neglected. The free *jogi* are themselves names of diseases: *jok kulu* causes miscarriage; *jok rubanga* is responsible for tuberculosis of the spine, etc. The *jok* in the head of the witch explains his anti-social behavior. He is the agent of the *jok*. In opposition to this, the *jok* in the diviner enables her to divine.

*Dominant Deities*

Although among the Central Luo the *jogi* are independent of each other, it is apparent that some of the Nilotic peoples have developed the concepts of dominant deities which seem to have a commanding influence over other deities. The *Kwoth* of the Nuer and the *Nhialic* of the Dinka are the best examples of these deities.

The Kenya Luo concepts of *Nyasaye* and *Were* seem to have been borrowed from the Luiya peoples, *Nyasaye* from the southern groups (Idaho, Kisa, Logoli, etc.) and *Were* from the northern groups (Wanga, Wagusu, etc.). When the Luo first arrived in their present-day country they found elements of Bantu and Lango peoples; but, according to Ogot, these people should not be identified with present Luiya peoples. [Ogot wrote,] "The pro-Luo inhabitants did not possess higher cultures, for, physical influences apart, they do not seem to have influenced the Luo culturally. In fact, in most cases, they have adopted Luo culture and language."[123] The contact between the Luo and Luiya peoples intensified as more immigrants arrived from Uganda during the seventeenth and eighteenth centuries, and this inevitably led to a policy of extension. It was probably at this period that the Luo acquired the concepts of *Nyasaye* and *Were* as well as the territory of the Luiya.

Whisson wrote, "But whatever its source, the concept of a creator spirit was present in the minds of the Luo before the introduction of the Christian concept of creator."[124]

The best proof of the Luiya origin of these concepts is that they are not known among the Central and Northern Nilotes. And unless it can be shown that the concepts were developed before the Luo came in contact with the Luiya, we can take it for granted that these were Luiya deities. *Jok rubanga* is another example of deities from a non-Nilotic source, and is known only among the Central Luo who received it from the Nyoro. This deity is unknown among the Northern Nilotes and also among the Kenya Luo.

Christian missionaries adopted the term *Nyasaye* as a name for the Christian God. And the myths collected by Wagner from the Luiya people about this deity indicate a strong biblical influence. In one of them we read that *Wele* (or *Were*) first created a man called Mwambu and later a woman by the name Sala (Sarah?). At first the two lived together without a child because "Mwambu did not know his wife," but later Sala got pregnant and gave birth to some children. God created the rainbow to stop rain, and also forbade men from eating certain creatures. The story ends, "God completed the whole work in six days. On the seventh day he rested, because it was a bad day."[125]

The Kenya Luo speak of *Nyasaye Nyakalaga*, meaning Nyasaye who is found in many places.[126] This has been interpreted by the missionaries as meaning the omnipresence of this deity. One curious aspect is that the word *Nyasaye* has a plural form *Nyiseche*. If, as the missionaries claim, *Nyasaye* is the one true God, how come that the word has a plural form? It seems that the Luo and Luiya peoples conceived of a category of deities singly known as *Nyasaye*, and collectively called *Nyiseche*.

Evans-Pritchard and Godfrey Lienhardt have intimated that the *Juok* of the Anuak and Shilluk were dominant deities. According to Evans-Pritchard, *Juok* is an all powerful and omnipresent spirit.[127] And Lienhardt wrote that the Shilluk *Juok* was one in essence, though, as it were, with many facets, which seem to refract him into a multitude of beings.[128] It should be pointed out that these remarks were not based on detailed field studies by these eminent scholars. Evans-Pritchard's book on the Anuak was only a preliminary survey, written after a very short visit to Anuakland; and Lienhardt's article was based solely on literary sources. But one suspects that even if the two anthropologists had done studies among the Anuak and Shilluk similar to their works among the Nuer and Dinka, respectively, their interpretations would still be basically the same, that is, in terms of the Christian God.

## Chiefdom Deities

The Central Luo and the Anuak call the "powers" to which they sacrifice at the chiefdom shrines, *jok* and *juok*, respectively. For the Anuak these are ghosts of important nobles, and it is the graves of these nobles which are the shrines. The Anuak believe that the ghosts appear in the form of snakes which haunt the vicinity of the graves. Some of the deities of the chiefdom shrines of the Central Luo are in the form of snakes, but they are not believed to be ghosts of important men. Others are "soil" from the supposed "original" country, rocks believed to have fallen from the sky, etc.

These concepts correspond with the Shilluk idea of *Nyikang*, and the Dinka concept of *Deng*. But it is striking that the Nuer and the Kenya Luo do not have the equivalent of chiefdom deities and shrines. As regards the Nuer the absence of chiefdom deities is in line with their political system with its lack of any central government organizations and the absence of legal institutions and political leadership. Aristotle wrote many years ago, "Wherefore men say that the Gods have a king, because they themselves either are or were in ancient times under the rule of a king. For they imagine, not only the forms of the Gods, but their ways of life to be like their own."[129] Where there are no chiefs there can be no chiefdoms, and also no chiefdom deities.

The development of chiefships and chiefdoms among the Kenya Luo seems to have taken place only recently. Evans-Pritchard wrote in 1936 that there was nothing that would be described as a political office among them. The *ruoth* was an influential person but no more.[130] Ogot has criticized this statement on the ground that it failed to appreciate the incipient chiefship that was beginning to emerge during the latter part of the nineteenth century. He wrote, "This period represents the formative era of Luo history during which they changed from being hordes of nomads moving about with their livestock in search of pasture and water, to sedentary societies with a recognizable way of life.[131]" But the institution of *ruoth*, chief, among the Kenya Luo, never developed into anything like the *rwot*, chief, among the Central Luo. And by the time the effects of colonial rule had begun to be felt by the Kenya Luo, the chiefship had not yet become established as a political institution, and the chiefdom deities had not yet been conceived.

*Ancestral Ghosts*

All the Nilotes referred to the ghosts of their ancestors as *jok*. These were generally regarded as benevolent, but their importance differed with different groups. Among the Central Luo the cult did not play a major role in the everyday life of the people. The shrines were neglected for months, and fell into disrepair; when clansmen gathered to offer sacrifices to the ancestors, the feast was fittingly called *yubbu abila*, repairing the shrine. The Nuer, likewise, pay little attention to the ghosts of the dead except when they are directly concerned with what is happening and their relationship with the living has to be emphasized; for example during a funeral or settlement of blood feuds started on account of their violent deaths, or the marriage of their children. The Nuer ancestral ghosts are associated with the post-shrine, *riek*, but the shrine is firstly erected to *Kwoth* as guardian of the homestead. No prayers are addressed to them because they have no powers in themselves to grant requests.[132]

It is important to distinguish between what Leinhardt has called the "clan divinities" of the Dinka and the ancestral ghosts. The former are embodied in totemic objects [....] These are respected and invoked when danger threatens; but the Dinka also have a cult of ancestors. Both the totemic objects and the ancestral ghosts are called *jok*.

*Pestilences, Murrains, etc.*

The word *jok* is also the name for plagues, pestilences, murrains and many other serious sicknesses. Among the Central Luo they are believed to be caused by *gemo*, a host of dwarfs which travel by night. On passing through the villages they punish the people if there is much hatred or jealousy in that village, by causing them to suffer in a particular way.

It is clear from the above summary that *jok* is not one thing but many and different things or powers. Claims that *jok* is the Supreme Being do not seem to be based on any concrete evidence, and must be rejected.

# HELLENIZATION OF AFRICAN DEITIES

When students of African religions describe African deities as eternal, omnipresent, omnipotent, omniscient, etc., they intimate that African deities have identical attributes with those of the Christian God. In other words, they suggest that Africans hellenized their deities, but before coming into contact with Greek metaphysical thinking. In this chapter this claim is rejected as absurd and misleading. And to do this it is necessary to trace briefly the development of the Christian God.

Christianity, like Islam, derives its monotheism from Judaism. JHVR or Yahweh was at first only one of many deities of ancient Jews.[133] It appears that it was during the period of captivity in Babylon that this deity emerged as the chief God. Jeremiah and Ezekiel seem to have invented the idea that all other deities except JHVR were false, and that he punishes idolatry.

> Therefore now thus saith the Lord, the God of hosts, the God of Israel, Wherefore commit ye this great evil against your souls, to cut off from you man and woman, child and suckling, out of Judah, to leave you none to remain; In that ye provoke me unto wrath with the works of your hands, burning incense unto other gods in the land of Egypt ... as I have punished Jerusalem, by the sword, by the famine, and by the pestilence. ... Then all the men which knew that their wives had burnt incense unto other gods, and all the women that stood by, a great multitude, even all the people that dwelt in the land of Egypt, in Pathros, answered Jeremiah, saying, "As for the word that thou hast spoken unto us in the name of the Lord, we will not harken unto thee. But we will certainly do whatever thing that goes forth out of our own mouth, to burn incense unto the queen of heaven, and to pour out drink offerings unto her, as we have done, we, and our fathers, our kings, and our princes, in the cities of Judah, and in the streets of Jerusalem: for then we had plenty of victuals, and were well."[134]

In 334 BCE, Alexander the Great conquered Darius III, the last of the Persian kings and the Jews became part of the Greek empire. Alexander was bent on extending Greek culture, and to achieve this he employed sex. He ordered his officers and men to intermarry with native populations and to beget many children. Within ten years he founded five Greek cities in the Middle East, the most important of which was Alexandria. In 175 BCE, a Seleucid king, Antioch IV, who was determined to hellenize all his dominions, established a school in Jerusalem, and young Jews were taught to wear Greek hats and practice athletics. There was a strong opposition to all this from a nationalistic party called the Hasidim (The Holy). In 170 BCE the Jews rebelled. Antiochus now resolved to destroy the Jewish religion, to stop circumcision and the custom of not eating pork. He identified JHVR with the Greek deity Zeus, took the holy vessel from the Temple and placed in it the image of the Greek deity. "They put to death certain women that had caused their children to be circumcised. And they hanged the infants about their necks, and rifled their houses, and slew them that circumcised them. How be it many in Israel were fully resolved and confirmed in themselves not to eat an unclean thing, wherefore they chose rather to die, that they may not be defiled with meats, and that they may not profane the holy covenant; so then they died."[135]

Judas Maccabaeus led the Jews in their revolt against Antiochus. He recaptured Jerusalem in 164 BCE and then extended the Jewish state by conquering Samaria and Joppa and Akra. In his conquests he sometimes killed all the males or circumcised them by force.

If most of the Jews rejected Greek culture, Greek philosophy was very readily absorbed by Jewish thinkers. The most well known of these was the philosopher Philo-Judaeus of Alexandria who was a contemporary of Jesus Christ. He set himself to reshape Platonic and Stoic teaching in the pattern of Jewish belief and tradition. He identified JHVR with the Logos, and paved the way for the Christian Fathers to reconcile Greek philosophy with the acceptance of Hebrew scriptures.[136]

The Jewish religion was very simple, involving nothing metaphysical. The "Good News" was about the coming of a Messiah who would bring them earthly prosperity and victory over their enemies. The "other-worldliness" of Jewish religion is a conception which, in a sense, resembles Platonism. The Greek teaching was that the sensible world, in space and time, is an illusion; and that by intellectual and moral discipline, a man can live in the eternal world of "ideas" which alone is real. But the Jewish doctrine does not conceive the Other World metaphysically. Rather, it is in the future, when men and women who have lived good and virtuous lives will enjoy everlasting bliss, while the sinful and the wicked will roast forever in the place below.

The Christians identified the Messiah with the historical Jesus; and, to begin with, Christianity was preached by Jews to Jews as reformed Judaism. Jewish Christianity was deeply entangled in Messianism. It was confidently expected that Christ would shortly return to earth, and assisted by angelic hosts, overthrow the Roman Empire and establish a theocracy at Jerusalem. For the first Christians heaven was just above the clouds, and that was where Jesus was waiting. This was the meaning and significance of Christ's supposed resurrection and resurrection for them.

St. James and, to a certain extent, St. Peter wished Christianity to remain a purely Jewish faith. But St. Paul was determined to admit the so-called Gentiles without even demanding circumcision or submission to Mosaic Law. Inge commented, "The religion of Christ was now taking a wider sweep, to embrace the whole Greco-Roman world without favor or distinction. And without knowing it, the church at this point turned her back, once and for all, on the East. From that day to this she has nothing to boast of outside the range of Roman–Roman culture. The success of Mohammedanism… marks the revolt of the Semite people against a religion which they were unable to understand. Christianity had won Europe and lost Asia."[137]

The catholicization of Christianity led to its becoming Hellenic, because the Greeks thought in metaphysical form. Thus in the Fourth Gospel, written about a hundred years after Christ, Jesus is identified with the Platonic-Stoic Logos. "In the beginning was the *Word*, and the *Word* was with God, and the word was God. All things were made by him, and without him was not anything made that was made. … And the *Word* was made flesh, and dwelt among us, and we beheld his glory, the glory of the only begotten of the Father, full of grace and truth."[138]

The rendering of this metaphysical poem into the Luo language bears testimony to the fact that the Nilotes, like the early Jews, do not think metaphysically. The concept of *Logos* does not exist in Nilotic thinking; so the word *Word* was translated into Lok which means news or message, as in the greeting "*Lok ango*?" ("What is the news?" or "How are you?") And, as the Nilotes were not very concerned with the beginning or the end of the world, the phrase, "In the beginning," was rendered, "*Nia con ki con*," which is, "From long long ago." We have already seen how the missionaries took the hunchback spirit as the equivalent of the creator.

The first verse of St. John's Gospel in Luo reads as follows: "*Nia con ki con Lok onongo tye, Lok tye bot Lubanga, Lok aye ceng Lubanga.*" Retranslated into English, it goes, "From long long ago there was News, News was with the Hunchback Spirit, News was the Hunch-back Spirit." Evans-Pritchard has lamented, "Missionaries have battled hard and with great sincerity to overcome these difficulties, but in my experience much of what they teach natives is quite unintelligible to those among whom they labor."[139] The crux of the matter is that it never occurred to the missionaries that Africans do not think metaphysically and that in any case, as the current debate within the Christian churches indicate, metaphysical thinking is perhaps a hindrance to the understanding of the nature of the deity.

Now, Jesus Christ and his twelve apostles spoke no Greek, and although he was probably a graduate of the Essenne Jesus was innocent of Greek philosophy.[140] He certainly did not identify himself with the *Logos*, and at his death he left no system of ethics or system of philosophy. The synthesis of Greek philosophy and Hebrew scripture was carried out by so-called Christian apologists, who, on the whole, were non-Jewish Christian converts trained to think in Hellenic terms. The professional philosopher Justin Martyr 100–167 CE; Theophilus, who, writing about 190 CE, was the first to use the concept of God as Trinity in Christian literature; the Anti-Gnostic fathers Irenaeus b. 130 CE and Tertullian b. 160 CE, Clement 150–213 CE and Origen d. 254 of the Alexandrian School, and St. Augustine 354–430 CE and others, were the men, who hellenized the conception of the Jewish deity JHVR into the Supreme Being, a Person or Trinity of Persons whose attributes were Omnipotence, Omnipresence, Eternity, etc.[141] And, as Leslie Dewart has remarked, "It would be inexact, therefore, to suppose that the Christian *theos* is the same as the Yahweh of the Old Testament."[142]

African deities have not undergone the process of hellenization that JHVR was subjected to. The Greek metaphysical ideas could not have occurred to African peoples before they came into contact with Greek philosophy. It follows that we cannot meaningfully speak of "Akan theology," because the term theology refers to that body of knowledge which can be obtained by human reason alone without the aid of revelation.[143] Abraham who talked about Akan theology badly contradicted himself when he wrote, "Indeed the Akan believed the knowledge of God to be intuitive and immediate. This is suggested by the adage ... 'No one teaches a child God.'"[144]

But Mbiti has confidently written, "In all these societies, without a single exception, people have a notion of God as the Supreme Being. This is the most minimal and fundamental idea about God, found in all African societies."[145] What does the term "Being" mean to African peoples? In scholastic philosophy God is conceived as *being* and this is based on the theory of knowledge of Parmenides 515–440 BCE. Briefly stated, it is that when you think you think of something, when you use a name it must be the name of something. And since you think and speak of it at one time as well as another, whatever can be thought or spoken of must exist at all times.[146] The Greek metaphysical tradition never doubted the existence of *intelligible reality*, or the reliability of knowledge, because in addition to the postulates of Parmenides, it assumed that being necessarily existed. Moreover, hellenization introduced into Christianity the ideas of immutability, stability, and impassibility as the central perfections of God. The Christian God was therefore described as the Supreme Being, because no other being could be greater than Him.

According to Danquah, the Akan title *Borebore* given to their deity means excavator, hewer, carver, creator, originator, inventor, architect. The Akan, we are told, describe the universe as having its architectural origin and form from God.[147] Here we catch Danquah, red-handed, trying to smuggle Platonic ideas into Akan thinking when he talks about the "architectural origin and form" of the universe. But, of course, the concept of creation *ex nihilo* has nothing in common with the meaning of the title *Borebore*. A creation out of nothing reveals a power greater than a creation out of something already there. In saying that God created the universe out of nothing, Christian theologians are, at the same time, commenting on God's omnipotence.

Omnipotence implies *infinite* power, not merely the power of clearing the forest, as the Ngombe of the Congo describe their deity; the great equatorial forest that once covered most of East Africa has been almost completely destroyed by man. Nor does the term mean having the power of "bending even majesties," which a political mob or an assassin can easily effect.[148]

African peoples may describe their deities as "strong" but not "omnipotent"; "wise," not "omniscient"; "old," not "eternal"; "great," not "omnipresent." The Greek metaphysical terms are meaningless in African thinking. Like Danquah, Mbiti, Idowu, Busia, Abraham, Kenyatta, Senghor and the missionaries, modern Western Christian anthropologists are intellectual smugglers. They are busy introducing Greek meta-physical conceptions into African religious thought. The African deities of the books, clothed with the attributes of the Christian God, are, in the main, creations of the students of African religions. They are all beyond recognition to the ordinary Africans in the countryside.

# DE-HELLENIZING THE CHRISTIAN GOD

What did African scholars find so beautiful and useful in Greek metaphysics that they chose it to be the vehicle for expressing African religious concepts? It would appear that African scholars were attracted to this tool not because of its usefulness or efficiency. They were reacting against intellectual arrogance, and, as Mazrui has put it, "In order to establish her intellectual equality with the West, Africa has to master Western versions of intellectual skills. Africa has to be as Greek as the next person."[149] And, while the West is busy demolishing the Hellenic moulds in which the Christian faith had become imprisoned, African scholars are busy collecting the same rusty, throwaway pieces and putting them on African deities.[150]

A commission set up by the Church of England in 1943 found that there was a wide gulf between the church and the people, and that only a small percentage of the nation joined regularly in public worship of any kind. It also reported the collapse of Christian morality. But the report threw the blame for all this on Humanism, which it described as "the age-long life."[151] Dewart has noted that the fairly total and serene self-assurance which has long characterized the Catholic believer has been shaken, and that there is unrest among the faithful and the clergy.[152] "All the landmarks are disappearing," Warren lamented. "Everywhere there is a desperate search for some inner basis of security, some inner assurance which can enable man to face the storm."[153]

There may be sociological and historical explanations for the turmoil within the Christian churches. But at the core of it is the revolution in philosophy which has resulted in the decline of metaphysical theology. In 1899 Pope Leo XII wrote the Encyclical Aeterni Patris in which he urged Roman Catholic philosophers to draw their inspiration from St. Thomas Aquinas, whose philosophy is regarded by the Catholic church to be the Christian philosophy par excellence. Leo judged Aquinas to be the prince of all the Catholic Doctors, and argued that his judgment has been supported by popes, general councils, universities and even by many outside the church. "We exhort you, Venerable Brethren, in all earnestness to restore the golden wisdom of St. Thomas, and to spread it far and wide for the defense and beauty of the Catholic faith, for the good of society, and for the advantage of all the sciences."[154]

This passionate plea was provoked by the steady decline of scholastic philosophy of the time. Towards the end of the nineteenth century it had become a mere "shadow of its golden, medieval self."[155] In the secular universities of France and Italy the study of philosophy was being more and more confined to the simple history of philosophical systems. The political and social life of Europe was dominated by dominant schools of secular philosophy. "The fires of philosophical theology and anti-theology were already burning low by the last decades of the nineteenth century," wrote Gilbert Ryle. "...In the middle of the 1920s they were out. ... Lecture halls, laboratories, and common rooms were occupied by theoretical discussions of a new kind. The theological imbroglios that stimulate philosophy came out of the work not of Renan, Newman or Colenso, but of such people as Cantor, Clerk, Maxwell, Mendel, Karl Marx, and Freud."[156]

The formal revolt against "Idealism" or metaphysical thinking, and the defense of common sense began at the beginning of this century, led by G. E. Moore, Bertrand Russell and Ludwig Wittgenstein.[157] Metaphysics which covered such allegedly philosophical enterprises as the attempt to describe *reality* as a whole, or to find the *purpose* of the Universe, or to reach beyond the everyday world to some supra-sensible spiritual order, was condemned as being literally nonsensical. According to the strictures of the *verification principle* the meaning of a statement is determined by the way it can be verified, where its being verified consists in its being tested by empirical observation. It follows then that statements like those of metaphysics of which no empirical observation could possibly be relevant, are ruled out as factually meaningless.[158] Bertrand Russell wrote, "Most philosophers… profess to prove, by *a priori* metaphysical reasoning, such things as the fundamental dogmas of religion, the essential rationality of the universe, the illusoriness of matter, the unreality of all evil, and so on. There can be no doubt that the hope of finding reason to believe such theses as these has been the chief inspiration of many life-long students of philosophy. This hope, I believe, is vain. It would seem that knowledge concerning the universe as a whole is not to be obtained by metaphysics, and that the proposed proofs that, in virtue of the laws of logic, such and such things *must* exist, and such and such others cannot, are not capable of surviving a critical scrutiny."[159] In 1925 Ramsay observed, "Most of us would agree that the objectivity of *good* was a thing we had settled and dismissed with the existence of God. Theology and Absolute Ethics are two famous subjects which we have realized have no real objects."[160]

The reactions of Christian thinkers to this devastating revolution may be grouped under two heads. First the Catholic church, which, as we have seen, has decided, in the manner of the captain of velour, to stay in the ship of metaphysical theology, although it appears to be sinking. Gilson Eteinne (b. 1884), the historian of philosophy and perhaps the most articulate exponent of Thomistic metaphysics, has warned Catholics against the hurried judgment that philosophical novelty is the only hope of the Christian in the contemporary world, because novelties come and go. Despite mistakes which lead to skepticism, every instance of the death of philosophy has been accompanied by renewal. Again, man, though disappointed by what he has been offered, returns to metaphysics as if by nature, for he seeks the first principle of what he experiences. For him, patience, docility and trust in the church are required if one is to be a Christian.[161]

Jacques Maritain (b. 1882) has sought to make the principles of St. Thomas Aquinas viable to the twentieth century. His *Degree of Knowledge* (1932) sets out to vindicate the relevance of Thomistic synthesis of knowledge and being for modern thought. Thomism is represented not as a system to be arbitrarily imposed on science, philosophy and theology, but as a flexible, pragmatic attitude toward material and spiritual realities. Knowledge on all levels, he tells us, depends on the process of abstraction; and for him, there are three levels of knowledge: that of experimental science where objects can neither exist nor be conceived without matter and thus must be viewed according to the verifiable properties. Objects on this level cannot be known "in themselves" or in their essence.

Second, the level of purified "sciences of explanation" like mathematics which refer to objects which, although existing in material form, can be conceived in abstraction from matter. Third, that of metaphysics, which involves objects which can be conceived without matter and may even exist without it, objects such as the quality of beauty and being.[162]

But even within the Catholic fold there are powerful dissenting voices. Leslie Dewart, for instance, has charged that the hellenization of the Christian faith has not only resulted in certain inadequacies but has also stultified Catholic philosophical thinking. Since the middle of the Middle Ages, he pointed out, Catholic thought has not contributed much to man's understanding of himself or of reality. He also attributed the condition of the possibility of modern atheism to the hellenization of Christianity. "If the prospect of integrating faith and contemporary experience is to be ultimately successful it must be sufficiently radical. And to be sufficiently radical it must get to the root concept of God. And to be sufficiently radical respecting the concept of God it must radically depart from the philosophical world-view which has given the traditional faith in God a cultural form which no longer serves well that faith."[163]

Many Protestant theologians admit openly that metaphysical theology is in a poor state. Ninian Smart has called it "the sick man of Europe."[164] Howard Root wrote, "It is possible that in their time the Five Ways (Thomas Aquinas' five 'proofs' of the existence of God) were an exciting expression of the whole movement from the actual world to the reality of God. ... But there can be no doubt that they no longer express anything of the sort."[165] The Protestant reaction which began with Rudolf Bultman, Dietrich Bonhoeffer, Paul Tillich, and Karl Barth developed into a near stampede in 1963 with the publication of John Robinson's *Honest to God*.[166]

Bultman set himself the task of "demythologizing" the Gospel. He asked such questions as, "Did the things we read in the Gospel really happen?" "Did Jesus really say the things he is reported to have said?" "And, anyway, is it truth for us today?" Bultman sought to find out what in the bible is kernel, and what is husk.[167] Bonhoeffer declared, "In a world thus come of age, man could live without the tutelage of God"; but he was hanged by the Nazis before he could suggest more concretely what form Christian theism might take once God was removed from the altar.[168] Paul Tillich has argued that the word "God" should be replaced by "Ground of Being" or "Ultimate Concern";[169] and in his discussion on "The Revelation of God and the Abolition of Religion," Barth has urged the abolition of religion itself, because, in contrast to revelation, which is God's self-offering, religion is a "grasping which is not true reception." [Barth wrote,] "If man believed, he would listen, but in religion he talks. If he believed, he would accept a gift; but in religion he takes something for himself. If he believed, he would let God himself intercede for God; but in religion he ventures to grasp at God."[170]

For the total demolition of the Hellenic mould which is now a hindrance rather than a help to the Christian faith, we return to the Catholic philosopher Leslie Dewart. He suggests, first of all, that Christian theism of the future might not conceive God as *being*, as it is in scholastic philosophy. He argues that if reality is not assumed to be constituted by intelligibility or by any relation to mind, reality can no longer be identified with *that-which-is* (which is the usual meaning of *being*). And since God is not a *being*, God cannot be said to *exist*. And since essence is proper to the *being* of creatures then God has no essence. And if God is not a being he is not an object of thought and has no definition or meaning as a *thing-in-itself*. And, in the same style, Dewart proceeds to demolish the concept of God as a Person or Trinity of Persons, and of the omnipotence, omnipresence, omniscience, eternity, and immutability of God; and, finally, even the name God itself is thrown out. "It is truly not a 'holy' name," he argues, "and it is man's, not God's invention." It is suggested that in the future it might become increasingly possible for the Christian faith to reserve a special place for silence in discourse about God. "We may learn that to say certain things well it is sometimes better to leave them unsaid."[171]

After almost two thousand years in the metaphysical wilderness[—]where the business of religion is a department of life separated from the rest of living, of religion, which, as Samuel Johnson wrote, "It is in a book: we have an order of men whose duty it is to teach: we have one day in the week set apart for it, and this is pretty well observed...."[—]Western man is beginning to return to the situation similar to those existing in many African societies.[172] John Taylor has called the Christian religion as practiced in Africa "Classroom Religion," and likened it to a girl's school uniform, "something to be put on at certain times and in particular circumstances, and has nothing to do with other areas of life."[173]

John Mbiti has observed, "Because traditional religions permeate all the departments of life, there is no formal distinction between the sacred and the secular, between the religious and non-religious, between the spiritual and the material areas of life. Wherever the African is, there is his religion." He noted that many African languages do not have a word for *religion*; "it nevertheless accompanies the individual from long before his birth to long after his physical death."[174]

In his book, *Men Without God?*, Keith Russell posed the question whether it is necessary that the church should insist on the autonomous existence of a department of life called "religion" which has a primarily metaphysical reference, and whether the accusation of "materialism" which the Western church so frequently brings against both its own people and the young African nations depends on a true understanding of the material in God's world, or if it is a hangover from centuries of insistence on a false sacred secular antithesis.

It has been intimated that, because religion permeates every aspect of life in African societies, there were no African non-believers in traditional Africa. As Mbiti explained, "A person cannot detach himself from the religion of his group, for to do so is to be severed from his roots, his foundation, his contact of security, his kinship, and the entire group of those that make him aware of existence. ... Therefore, to be without religion amounts to a self-excommunication from the entire life of society; and African peoples do not know how to exist without religion."[175] For Mbiti, of course, religion includes beliefs concerning God and the spirits, as well as the rituals that an individual undergoes from before his birth until after his death.

Karl Heim has argued that although secularism has existed in ancient times, in its present form it is a product of that area of the world which was influenced by the biblical view of the relationship between God, man and the world.[176] [For him,] "Secularism is the possibility man has of abstracting himself from God and the question of eternity; of regarding them as an 'ideological superstructure'; and of attempting to be a child of this world."[177]

Now, although attempts have been made to describe certain African deities in terms of the attributes of the Christian God, all of them are actually continuously and geographically present and intimately concerned with the day-to-day life of the people, here on earth. No genuinely metaphysical speculations are attached to them, and there is no thought of another world. It follows then that, in so far as Africans believed in certain "powers," they may be called religious; but, as most of them did not hold beliefs in any deities similar in conception to the Christian God, we may refer to traditional Africans as atheistic in their outlook.

It is this which has provoked Keith Russell to comment that the early death of Dietrich Bonhoeffer was no great loss to the Acholi. The German theologian had written from prison that God was teaching men that they must live as people who could get along very well without him. The Acholi had no need to be taught anything like this, they knew it very well already. Moreover in the Acholi worldview men have learned to cope with all questions of importance without recourse to a God as a working hypothesis. And even in death the Acholi need no God. This is the meaning of this profound funeral poem that they sing at the last funeral ceremony.

> Fire rages at Layima
> Fire rages in the valley
> Of river Cumu,
> Everything is utterly utterly destroyed;
>
> If I could reach
> The homestead of Death's mother
> O! my daughter
> I would make a long grass torch,
> If I could reach
> The homestead of Death's mother
>
> I would destroy everything utterly utterly
> Like the fire that rages at Layima
> Like the fire that rages
> In the valley of river Cumu!

# Some Conclusions

What emerges from this brief survey is a distorted and pale picture of African religious beliefs, their deities buried under thick layers of the prejudices of the students of African societies. Throughout the long history of Western scholarship African religions have never been the object of study in their own right. African deities were used as mercenaries in foreign battles, not one of which was in the interest of African peoples.

The Homeric poems which described Africans and their deities so laudably were, in fact, commentaries on, and criticisms of, the aristocracy of Greece of that time, and their deities. Gilbert Murray described the Olympian gods as follows, "The gods of most nations claim to have created the world. The Olympians make no such claim. The most they ever did was to conquer it.... And when they have conquered their kingdoms, what do they do? Do they attend to the Government? Do they promote agriculture? Do they practice trade and industries? Not a bit of it. Why should they do honest work? They find it easy to live on the revenues and blast with thunder bolts the people who do not pay. They are conquering chieftains, royal buccaneers. They fight, and feast, and play, and make music; they drink deep and roar with laughter at the lame smith who waits on them. They are never afraid, except of their own king. They never tell lies except in love and war."[178] It was against these tough, fighting and drunken deities and the Greek leaders whom they reflected that the poets sang, contrasting them with what they imagined were African deities and African peoples.

When St. Augustine shouted insults at the gods of his father by calling them demons, he was in the heat of battle, firstly against his own "pagan" background from which he wished to escape into Christianity, and secondly in the great theological debates which shaped the form of the Christian faith.[179] "All the gods of the gentiles are demons" was a battle cry shouted by one of the greatest generals of the new and aggressive religious army whose undisguised aim was to conquer the whole world as the founder of the faith is reported to have commanded, "Go ye unto all the world and preach the gospel unto all creatures."[180] The Christian Fathers had no intention of presenting African deities as they really were. Their main aim was to condemn and then destroy what they called "demons," and replace them with the Christian faith.

We hear echoes of the same battle cry from the fifteenth century onwards, when hordes upon hordes of barbarians from Europe disguised as Christians leapt from ships, bible and gun in hand, to attack, plunder, murder and enslave the inhabitants of the whole world. The writers of that long period of Western domination set out to justify the colonial system by preaching that the world was sick and needed Western suppression (re-christened civilization), in order to survive. The speculations of the eighteenth century philosophers and those of the nineteenth century anthropologists were not meant to give a true picture of African religions. These people were not interested in a proper study of African societies, because if they were, they would have come to Africa to carry out researches. Their works were "apologies" for the colonial system: their task was to demonstrate the superiority of Western culture over those of the colonized peoples.

African deities fared no better at the hands of the philosophers who talked of the noble savage, because, like the Homeric poets, they were engaged not in studying African religions but in criticizing their own societies, using the same principle which, in northern Uganda, is expressed in the saying that "every married woman thinks that the husbands of the other women are less troublesome than hers." The terms such as "Fetishism" and "Animism," which were coined and used by Western writers in their imaginary speculations, are not only meaningless, they are a nuisance in the proper understanding of African religions. They must be dropped.

For the first time in Western scholarship, the systematic study of African religions through fieldwork began about forty or so years ago. A golden opportunity presented itself for the recording and understanding of African religious conceptions as they really are. But, alas, the materials collected from these researches have been interpreted in such a way that African deities became distorted beyond recognition. And, once more, African religious conceptions were drafted by Christian scholars to fight on their side against European non-believers. The Hellenic armors with which African deities were clothed were not primarily for their protection, but to make them appear like the Christian God. Their great number was greatly publicized and used to frighten the "enemy."

The first duty of an African scholar is to remove these rusty Greek metaphysical dressings as quickly as possible, before African deities suffocate and die inside them in the same manner as the Christian God had perished. Because, now, when Christian theologians try to break open the Hellenic coffin in which the Christian God was imprisoned, he is no longer to be seen. Fritz Mauthner has proclaimed, "God is dead. The time has come to write his history."[181]

Kimball has written, "The scientific interest in religion of half a century ago seems to have dwindled among anthologists, although a few sociologists are now evincing an interest in its social aspects. Occasionally essays on the subject emerge in the literature of social science, but the field has been left almost entirely to theologians." And Evans-Pritchard commented rather sadly, "While in other departments of anthropology, some, even considerable, advance has been made by intensive research in the study of kinship and political institutions, for example, I do not think that comparable advance has been made in the study of primitive religion."[182] The reasons for the decline of the study of African religions among anthropologists are not difficult to see. First, this is part of the general decline of social anthropology as a subject. Born to serve the practical needs of the colonial system, it was bound to die with the system. M. Fortes stated, "Various Colonial governments encouraged and assisted important anthropological researches which could not otherwise have been possible. The flood of government largesse we have had since the war (now, alas, coming to an end) could not have been foreseen in 1939, let alone in 1904. It behooves us to remember with all the more gratitude the support given to anthropological studies by governments of British overseas territories in the past. They helped to make a concern with the practical values of our research a characteristic of British anthropology."[183] In 1965 Aidan Southall noted that both the resources and younger scholars engaged in social anthropology showed serious signs of falling away.[184] The "flood of government largesse" was drying up because the British colonial empire was no more.

The second reason for the decline in the study of African religious beliefs is that the burning theological debates in the West have now ended. African deities which had been used as mercenaries have become redundant. But the missionaries, seeing another chance to convert Africa at the time of *uhuru*, have redoubled their efforts in the study of African religions. In my opinion they are bound to fail, because, like the earlier missionaries, they have stubbornly stuck to the misconceptions of the earlier writers, and secondly, because they are busy dressing African deities in Hellenic metaphysical husks which have been discarded by the Christian God. These preoccupations leave the proper study of African religions untouched.

*Some Pitfalls*

We have noted that Western Christian anthropologists confess openly that, in their interpretation of African religions, they are influenced by their own cultural backgrounds. A similar excuse has been used by John Mbiti, who argued that, philosophy of one kind or another was behind the thinking and acting of every people, and a study of traditional religions brought us into those areas of African life, where through word and action, we might be able to discern the philosophy behind. [Mbiti wrote,] "This involves interpretation of the information before us, and interpretation cannot be completely free of subjective judgment. What therefore is 'African Philosophy,' may not amount to more than simply my own process of philosophizing the items under consideration; but this cannot be helped, and in any case I am by birth an African."[185] The writer did not add that he was also a Christian theologian and a priest, which is more important, as what comes out of his works are more Christian than African. Students who desire to understand African religions as they are must reject this approach entirely. The protests by Evans-Pritchard, Godfrey Lienhardt and Mbiti against the non-Christian interpretation of religion are against the subjective approach of those scholars. We must reject all forms of subjectivity whether the subjectivity arises from anti-Christian, or from pro-Christian prejudices.

Certain assumptions deriving from Christian theology—that amalgam of Platonic and Aristotelian ways of thinking and Judaic concepts and Christian claims—ought not to be brought in when Christian students approach the study of African religion. First, the assumption that the universe is purposive throughout. St. Thomas's "Fifth Proof" of the existence of God was that we find even lifeless things serving a purpose, which must be that of some being outside them, since only living things can have an internal purpose. Christian anthropologists and missionaries have written as though this were also true of the beliefs of African peoples. But there is no evidence that African peoples see a purpose in all things. Indeed, most of the religious activities in African religions seem to be part of the ways and means of dealing with existing or threatening dangers. In African thinking the universe seems to consist of three categories of objects, namely:
    (a) Useful objects, e.g., foodstuff, tools, weapons, etc.
    (b) Harmful objects, e.g., snakes, diseases, poisons, etc.
    (c) Neutral objects, e.g., stars—except those that guide a lost hunter; numerous types of harmless insects, millipedes, lizards, toads, etc.

The purpose of any particular object is determined by its use to human beings, and not "of some being outside them." Even the deities are there to serve the interests of men. The African deities are for man, and not man for them.

The second Christian assumption which should be left behind is that the temporal order of nature is in some sense inferior and illusory. This is the basis of the other-worldliness of the Christian faith. It seems that there is no other-worldliness in African religious thought. African ethics is not grounded on a promise or threat by some God that the good people will, in the future, enjoy life in heaven, while the bad will cook in a great fire. In this sense, the use of the term heaven in describing African religious concepts is confusing and misleading.

Some Ganda men told John Taylor, "My fire is my God, for it cooks the food I eat"; "Our God is our food and our pipes, nothing else"; "I know God, he made all things, but I don't want to worship him, you can teach the children." Taylor commented, "God, in spite of grace, has not yet been brought inside. Now Africa's century of acquiescence is coming to an end and the old views and values are reasserting themselves. If God remains outside much longer, African's this-worldliness will turn into materialism."[186] To Africans this is the only world, and it is neither inferior to any other, nor illusory.

The third Christian assumption which has misled many Christian students of African religion is that God is unknowable. The term knowledge as used in Christian theology is a metaphysical concept. St. Thomas Aquinas argued, "For the divine essence by its immensity surpasses every form to which our intellect reaches; and thus we cannot apprehend it by knowing what it is."[187] Mbiti wrote, "May God forgive me for attempting to describe him, and for doing it so poorly. Even if I am presenting here the wisdom and reflections of many African peoples, it is only at its best only an expression of a creature about the Creator. As such it is limited, inadequate and ridiculously anthropocentric. God is still beyond our human imagination, understanding, and expression."[188] Most African peoples know the names, abode and characteristics of their deities. They know them by the diseases they cause. The task of the diviner is, precisely, to determine which deity is responsible for a particular misfortune, and how to deal with it. In northern Uganda certain chiefdom deities were carried from place to place. The knowledge of Africans about their deities is not limited, inadequate or ridiculous in any way.

The last and most important pitfall for the Christian student is his belief in one God and the assumption which arises from it, namely that Africans must also have a High God. It is this assumption which has led Evans-Pritchard to interpret the numerous deities of the Nuer as refractions of God, and Placide Tempels to arrange the so-called "life-forces" of the Bantu in a hierarchy at the apex of which is the supposed High God. This also explains the preoccupation of many writers with some half-forgotten deities which are described as no longer interested in the affairs of men, and yet, they are called the High God. The aim of the study of African religions should be to understand the religious beliefs and practices of African peoples, rather than to discover the Christian God in Africa.

*Some Practical Issues*

African leaders and governments declare that the reconstruction of their societies will be based on African ideals and beliefs. Leopold Senghor wrote, "The antifederalists have accused us of being atheists, 'Marxists,' and of outlawing religion. Surely this smacks of propaganda. Can we integrate Negro-African cultural values, especially religious values, with socialism? We must answer that question once and for all with an equivocal yes."[189] Julius Nyerere has stated that African socialism "is rooted in our own past—in the traditional society which produced us. Modern African socialism can draw from its traditional heritage the recognition of 'society' as an extension of the family unit."[190] The Government of Kenya has presented its political thinking in the *Sessional Paper No. 10* of 1963–65. Paragraph 10 of that document reads, "Another fundamental force in African traditional life was religion which provided a strict moral code for the community. This will be a permanent feature of African socialism."

But will the African deities survive the revolutions in science and philosophy which have killed the Christian God? I doubt it. Christianity has declined because the Christian God used to fill gaps in science, or to deal with life at the point at which things got beyond human explanation or control. This has now been dismissed as intellectual laziness or superstition. The Christian God has become intellectually superfluous and, moreover, the metaphysical statements about him do not make sense to modern man.

In northern Uganda the chiefdom deities perished during the first few years of colonial rule. Today there are many young men and women who know nothing at all about them. The cult of ancestors is still strong, and this reflects the continuing bond of relationship between members of a clan. The numerous *jogi*, spirits, which are believed to be the cause of diseases and other misfortunes, appear to be on the increase.

The belief in these deities provides the explanations as well as the methods of dealing with misfortunes and ill-health. With the advance of medical knowledge, perhaps one day, the people of northern Uganda and other peoples of Africa will tell the diviners, in the words of Voltaire, "You have made ample use of the time of ignorance, superstition, and infatuation, to strip us of our inheritance, and strangle us under your feet, that you might fatten on the substance of the unfortunate. But tremble for fear that the day of reason will arrive."[191]

However, the important issue is not whether African deities and religions will or will not die out. It is a fact that the vast majority of Africans today hold the beliefs of their religions. Christianity has barely touched the core of the life of most African peoples. Keith Russell has estimated that in northern Uganda ninety percent of the homes still have connections with the clan rituals at times of need.[192] It seems to me that the new God of Christianity was taken by many African peoples as just another deity, and added to the long list of the ones they believed in. So that many African Christians are also practitioners of their own religions.

It follows that if the leaders sincerely believe that the social reconstruction in Africa should be based on the African worldview, their religions must be studied and presented as accurately as possible, so as to discover the African worldview. Christian sex ethics, its *other-wordiness*, and its preoccupations with sin are three important areas which African intellectuals and leaders can explore, because, here, Christianity contrasts vividly with African religions.

One of the basic issues of nation building is the concept of the *family*. Commissions of inquiry have been set up in many African countries to look into the question of marriage, indicating the unsatisfactory state of affairs resulting from the colonial marriage laws.[193] Otto Kahn-Freund wrote, "The great problem is that of the unification and codification of the law in a culturally and religiously plural society. How can the consciousness of the great strength of the social norms which hold them together be combined with the need for creating a modern, intelligible, unified system of law? How and where can one find the difficult path between an over-conservative and timid insistence on the tradition and diversity and an over-radical and unrealistic insistence on modernization and unity?"[194] The Kenya Commissioners, in their introduction to the Report on the Law of Succession, wrote, "We agreed that the law should generally be compatible with the African way of life, and should not be based on any foreign model. On the other hand, the law should recognize that the traditional African way of life is rapidly changing and should therefore cater for differing conditions both in the rural and urban areas. We thought that the law should recognize that Kenya is a country of many races, tribes, communities and religions, that the law and custom of these different people are deep-rooted and that any change we suggest should offend as little as possible their respective beliefs. On the other hand, we thought that the new law should encourage national unity and the building of Kenya as one nation irrespective of race or creed."[195]

It is suggested that these analyses do not go to the root of the problem, which is, the African idea of sex and marriage. Because it is this which the law should reflect. And, on the whole, there is a fundamental similarity in African sex values, and these differ very much from those of Christianity.

Despite the changes in the mental outlook which began with the renaissance, from when the authority of science began to increase at the expense of the authority of the church, and, in spite of the revolution led by Martin Luther who broke the chains of priestly celibacy, the Western world is still a prisoner of St. Paul's thwarted sexual morality. The nudist camps that are springing up all over the Western world, free love, the domination of the theater and the film industries by sex, and even the mini-skirt craze, are all, in the final analysis, protests against Saul of Tarsus.

This ex-Pharisee, who has been described as the "ugly little Jew," was a small man barely five feet tall, bow-legged, a chronic malarial patient with serious eye trouble. We learn from Acts, chapter IX that he became a mental case for a short time, and on recovery, he joined the Christians whom he had formerly persecuted. Paul was a great woman hater. He wrote to the Corinthians, "It is reported commonly that there is fornication among you, and such fornication as is not so much as named among the gentiles, that one should have his father's wife. And ye are puffed up, and have not rather mourned that he that hath done this deed might be taken away from among you. For I verily ... have judged already in the name of our Lord Jesus Christ ... to deliver such a one unto Satan for the destruction of the flesh, that the spirit may be saved in the day of Lord Jesus."[196]

What did Paul think of marriage? He wrote, "It is good for a man not to touch a woman. Nevertheless to avoid fornication, let every man have his own wife, and let every woman have her own husband. ... I say therefore to the unmarried and widows, it is good for them if they abide even as I, but if they cannot contain let them marry, for it is better to marry than to burn."[197]

It appears that it was the Pauline sex hatred rather than Christ's more humane attitude to women that became the basis of Christian morality. When certain people raised complaints because a prostitute had anointed him with an expensive perfume, he told his host, "I entered this thine house, thou gavest me no water for my feet: but she hath washed my feet with tears, and wiped them with the hair of her head. Thou gavest me no kiss, but this woman, since the time I came in hath not ceased to kiss my feet."[198] When another woman was brought to him, caught "in the very act" of committing adultery, and he was asked, "Now Moses in the law commanded us that such should be stoned; but what sayest thee?"

Jesus stooped down and began to write in the sand as though he heard them not. When they persisted with their questioning he replied, "He that is without sin among you, let him first cast a stone at her." The accusers left. Jesus told the woman, "Neither do I condemn thee: go and sin no more."[199]

He told Martha, who was jealous of her sister, "Martha, Martha, thou art troubled about many things. But one thing is needful: and Mary hath chosen that good part, which shall not be taken away from her."[200] Jesus attended a wedding party and supplied very good wine for the guests.[201] The women-hatred of Paul does not occur in the utterances of Jesus Christ.

The word *fornication* means voluntary sexual intercourse between two unmarried persons, or two persons not married to each other.[202] In most African societies, having sexual intercourse with married women by persons other than their husbands is strictly forbidden; but unmarried women enjoy both unmarried and married men. In northern Uganda mothers encourage their daughters to sleep with their boyfriends and test their manhood before marriage. When caught, a man pays the fornication fine called *luk*. This is nothing sinful or even shameful. Indeed, a man feels proud because of it. Taylor commented, "After the graduations of childhood, the wonder of sex maturing ties in the fact that by its means a boy or girl literally attains Manhood and becomes a link in the living chain of humanity. This newly quickened power is the most intensive expression of the life force and the young walk proudly... 'You are still a child,' you may say jokingly to a young girl. And softly but with immense confidence she may reply... 'I am older than that,' or, 'I have reached maturity,' or even, 'I am no longer a virgin.' For sex is good, and the joy of it goes far beyond its physical pleasures and outshines even the shame, which may be great, of breaking the bounds."[203] It is important for African leaders to consider whether sexual ethics in their countries should be based on St. Paul's prejudices against women and sex, or built on the African viewpoint which takes sex as a good thing.

*Political Philosophy*

The rejection of communism by most African leaders reflects not only their non-aligned stance in international politics. African leaders were repelled by the inhumanities of communism, and its totalitarian excesses. It is doubtful also whether the ultimate goal of communism—that "heaven" of communism, *when the state shall wither away*[—]was attractive and convincing enough. But most African countries profess to be socialistic. Even feudalists, rich landlords and businessmen, peasants and military chieftains, all call themselves socialists. This socialist sentiment in Africa is not based on the existence of a significant capitalist class. The political and economic revolutions are not thought to be led by a strong industrial proletariat. The slogan, "Working men of all the world unite..." does not sound right in predominantly peasant Africa.

African leaders identified imperialism with capitalism. The more radical elements within the nationalist movements turned to socialism both as aids in their struggle for *uhuru*, and in their thinking of the kind of society they would build. But their approach to Marxism was very selective and discriminating, borrowing only what suited their interests. On attaining *uhuru* African leaders are compelled by the desire to discover, within their own national traditions, the ideological and cultural inspiration for their political conceptions and social program. As a result there is a movement in many parties to turn to more indigenous ways and thinking. As Tom Mboya argued, "Each country has its own history, its own culture, its own inheritance of economic institutions and resources, and its own problems. To impose on a people a rigid system that takes no account of their needs, desires, aspirations and customs is to court disaster and failure."[204]

The most critical decisions which leaders of Africa must take lie not so much in the economic or political fields, but in the fields of culture and of basic human values. Of course there are conflicts between political philosophies and economic system; there is also the rivalry between power blocks. But the basic conflict is between fundamental assumptions of Western civilization and the fundamental assumptions of African civilization. The assumptions of Western man have their roots in Judaism, the Greek and Roman experiences, the Christian faith and industrialization. True *uhuru* means the abolition of Western political and economic dominance from Africa, and the reconstruction of our societies on the basis of African thought systems. The study of African religions is one important way of understanding African ways of thought.

# Selected Bibliography

Abbot, Walter, M. (ed.) *Documents of Vatican II*, New York, 1966.

Abraham, W. B. *The Mind of Africa*, London, 1962.

Abrahamsson, H. *The Origin of Death*, Uppsala, 1951.

Ajayi, Ade, T. F. and Espie (eds.) *A Thousand Years of West African History*, London, 1965.

——. *Christian Missions in Nigeria: the making of a new elite*, London, 1966.

Aristotle. *Politics*, in *The Works of Aristotle*, translated by Benjamin Jowett, Oxford, 1921.

Ayer, A. J. *Language, Truth and Logic*, London, 1946.

Ayer, A. J. *Political Essays*, London, 1966.

Banton, M. (ed.) *Anthropological Approach to the Study of Religion*, London, 1966.

Beattie, J. M. *Other Cultures*, London/New York, 1965.

Beetham, T. A. *Christianity and New Africa*, London, 1967.

Beier, Ulli *Origin of Life and Death: African creation myths*, London, 1966.

Bernheimer, Richard. *Wild men in the Middle Ages*, Cambridge, 1952.

Bottomore, T. B. (ed.) *Karl Marx's Writing*, London, 1963.

Busia, K. A. *Africa in search of Democracy*, London, 1967.

Butt, A. *The Nilotes of the Anglo-Egyptian Sudan and Uganda*, London, 1952.

Crazzolara, J. P. *The Lwoo*, 3 vols., Verona, 1950–3.

Crazzolara, J. P. *A study of the Acooli language*, London, 1938.

Cross, F. L. *The Early Christian Fathers*, London, 1960.

Danquah, J. B. *Akan Doctrine of God*, London, 1958.

Dawson, C. *Religion and the Rise of Western Culture*, New York, 1958.

D'Arcy, M. C. (ed.) *Thomas Aquinas: Collected Works*, London, 1939.

Dewart, L. *Future of Belief*, London, 1967.

Dimont, M. I. *Jews, God and History*, New York, 1962.

Diodorus. *Works*, translated by C. H. Oldfather, London, 1955.

Durkheim, E. *Elementary Forms of the Religious Life*, London, 1915.

Dutt, R. P. *Crisis of Britain and the British Empire*, London, 1957.

Eliade, M. *The Sacred and the Profane*, translated by William R. Trask, New York, 1957.

Eliade, M. *Patterns in Comparative Religion*, New York/London, 1958.

Evans-Pritchard, E. E. *Witchcraft, Oracles and Magic among the Azande*, Oxford, 1937.

——. *The Political System of the Anuak of the Anglo-Egyptian Sudan*, London, 1940.

——. *Theories of Primitive Religion*, London, 1940.

## SELECTED BIBLIOGRAPHY

——. *Essays in Social Anthropology*, 1962.

——. *Nuer Religion*, Oxford, 1956.

Fern V. (ed.) *A History of Philosophical Systems*, New York, 1950.

Fortes, M. *Social Anthropology in Cambridge since 1900*, Cambridge, 1952.

Frazer, Sir James. *The Golden Bough*, London, 3rd edition, 1919.

Freud, S. *The Future of an Illusion*, London, 1928.

——. *Civilization and its Discontents*, London, 1930.

Freidland, W. and Rosberg (eds.) *African Socialism*, Stanford, 1964.

Hanke, Lewis. *Aristotle and the American Indians*, Bloomington/London, 1970.

Herodotus. *The Histories*, translated by George Rawlinson, London, 1946.

Inge, W. R. "The Theology of the Fourth Gospel" *in Cambridge Biblical Essays*, London, 1909.

Katz, S. *The Decline and Fall of Rome and the Rise of Medieval Europe*, New York, 1967.

Kenyatta, J. *Facing Mount Kenya*, London, 1953.

Kerkhofs, J. *Modern Mission Dialogue*, New York/London, 1968.

Kihangirye, C. *The Marriage Customs of the Lango Tribe (Uganda) in Relation to Canon Law*, Rome, 1957.

Fulop-Miller, R. *Lenin and Gandhi*, London/ New York, 1927.

Lessa, W. and Vogt, E. Z. (eds.) *Reader in Comparative Religion*, New York, 1946.

Luibheid, C. *The Essential Eusebius*, New York, 1966.

Magill, F. N. (ed.) *Masterpieces of Catholic Literature: Essay-reviews of 300 great works Influential in Moulding the Catholic Faith*, New York, London, 1966.

Mair, L. *Primitive Government*, London, 1962.

Maritain, J. *Man and the State*, London, 1951.

——. *Moral Philosophy*, London, 1960.

Mazrui, A. *Ancient Greece in African Political Thought*, Nairobi, 1967.

Mbiti, John, S. *African Religions and Philosophy*, London/New York, 1969.

——. *Concepts of God in Africa*, London/New York, 1970.

——. *Poems of Nature and Faith*, Nairobi, 1969.

Mboya, T. J. *The Challenge of Nationhood*, London, 1970.

Montagu, A. *The Concept of the Primitive*, London/New York, 1968.

Morehead, A. *The White Nile*, London, 1960.

Muller, F. M. *Lectures on the Origin of Religion*, London, 1910.

Neill, S. *Colonization and Christian Mission*, London, 1966.

Parrinder, G. *African Traditional Religion*, London, 1963.

Pearce, H. *Savagism and Civilization*, Baltimore, 1967.

Ramsay, I. T. *Prospects for Metaphysics*, London, 1961.

Robinson, John A. *Honest to God*, London, 1963.

Roscoe, J. *The Baganda*, London, 1911.

Russell, B. *The Problems of Philosophy*, London, 1912, 1963.

Schmidt, M. *Primitive Races of Mankind*, translated by Alexander K. Dallas, Boston, 1929.

Senghor, L. S. *On Socialism*, London, 1964.

——. *Negritude et Humanisme*, Paris, 1964.

Shapiro, H. L. (ed.) *Man, Culture and Society*, New York, 1960.

Sinai, I. R. *Challenge of Modernisation*, London, 1964.

Smith, E. *African Ideas of God*, London, 1950.

Snowden, F. Jr. *Blacks in Antiquity: Ethiopians in the Greco-Roman Experience*, Cambridge (Mass), 1970.

Stephenson, J. *A New Eusebius*, London, 1957.

Stock, E. *History of the Church Missionary Society*, London, 1899.

Tanner, R. E. S. *Transition in African Belief*, Maryknoll/New York, 1967.

Taylor, J. *The Primal Vision*, London, 1963.

Temple, P. *Bantu Philosophy*, London, 1959.

Thomas, O. C. *Attitudes Towards other Religions*, New York, 1969.

Tillich, P. *The Shaking of the Foundation*, London, 1949.

Trevor-Roper, H. *The Rise of Christian Europe*, London, 1964.

Van Gennep, A. *Rites of Passage*, translated by Monica B. Vizedom and L. Gabrielle, Chicago, 1960.

Vidler, A. R. (ed.) *Soundings: Essays concerning Christian Understanding*, Cambridge, 1966.

Warren, M. A. C. *Introduction to the Primal Vision*, London, 1963.

Welbourn, F. B. and Ogot, B. A. *A Place to Feel at Home*, Oxford, 1966.

Welbourn, F. B. *East African Rebels*, London, 1961.

——. *East African Christian*, London, 1965.

Westerman, D. *The Shulluk People*, Berlin and Philadelphia, 1912, 1970.

Williams, E. *Capitalism and Slavery*, New York, 1966.

Wilson, C. J. *Uganda in the Days of Bishop Tucker*, London, 1955.

# Notes

*Note: All citations are that of the author and they appear largely unchanged from the original text. Only egregious errors have been corrected.*

1. Okot P'Bitek, *Song of Lawino* (Nairobi: East African Publishing House, 1966), 111-18.
2. *Capital*, vol.1, ch. 31.
3. Quoted by R. Palme Dutt, *The Crisis of Britain and the British Empire*, London, 1957, p. 69.
4. *Religion and the Rise of Western Culture*, New York, 1958, pp. 16-18.
5. See Stephen Neill, *Colonization and Christian Mission*, London, 1966, pp. 266-7.
6. *History of the Church Missionary Society*, London, 1899, vol. 1, p. 46.
7. *Capitalism and Slavery*, New York, 1966.
8. In 1871 the Ethnological Society and the Anthropological Society of 1860 were amalgamated to form the Royal Anthropological Institute of Great Britain and Ireland.
9. "Preface," *Transactions of the American Ethnological Society*, vol. 1, 1845, p. ix.
10. Max Schmidt, *Primitive Races of Mankind*, translated by Alexander K. Dallas, Boston, 1929, p. 19.
11. Sir John L. Myres, "A century of our work," *Man*, vol. 44, 1944, pp. 2-9.
12. See H. Bailey, "The role of Anthropology in Colonial Development," *Man*, vol. 44, 1944, pp. 10-16; Lucy Mair, "Applied Anthropology" in *Encyclopedia of Social Sciences*; Joan Vincent, "Anthropology and Political Development" in *Change in Developing Countries*, edited by Colin Leys, Cambridge, 1969.
13. *Man*, vol. 44, p. 1.
14. See Meyer Fortes, *Social Anthropology in Cambridge since 1900*, Cambridge, 1953, p. 3.
15. "Anthropological understanding of man," *Anthropological Quarterly*, vol. 32, January 1959, no. 1, p. 4.
16. M. Lewis, "Tribal Society" in *International Encyclopedia of Social Sciences*, pp. 146-150. But how the expression "tribal society" avoids or minimizes the moralistic overtones is not clear, since the term still means societies of peoples living in primitive or barbaric conditions.
17. *Lectures on the Early History of Institutions*, New York, 1888, pp. 72-4.
18. But note that K. Busia not only agrees with Main's speculations, he uses it to analyze what he calls the African political heritage. See *Africa in search of Democracy*, London, 1967, chap. 2.
19. Op. cit., p. 147.
20. "The structure of unilineal descent," *American Anthropologist*, vol. 53, no. 1, p. 18.
21. This means that in truly nomadic societies where there are no [proprietary] rights which can be asserted over defined areas of land, "tribe" in this strict sense does not exist.
22. See R. S. Anywar, *Acoli ki ker niegi*, Nairobi, 1954.
23. "Luo tribes and clans," [in] *The position of Women in Savage Societies and Other Essays*, New York, 1965, pp. 207-209. The others are Kano, Nyakach, Karachuonyo, Kadim, Kocia, Kanyala, Gem, Kanyamwa, Karungu, Kwbwai, Kanyadoto, Kakwae and Sakwa. Other locations are occupied by Bantu peoples who speak Luo only, Kagan and Mohoru, or speak Luo and their language: Kasigunga, Kaksingiri and Gwasi. A Luo group Wanjire have adopted a Bantu dialect and lost *dho-Luo*. Kamagambo and Kanyankago are of Lango origin.
24. *An introduction to Social Anthropology*, Oxford (first printed in 1965), 1967 edition, p. 12.

25 "'Political anthropology' the analysis of the symbolisms of power relations" in *Man*, New Series, vol. 4, no. 2, June 1969, pp. 230-31. See also Colin Leys, *Policies and Politicians: An essay on politics in Acholi*, Uganda, 1962-65, Nairobi, 1967, chap. 6.

26 Op. cit., p. 150.

27 *The Histories of Herodotus*, translated by George Rawlinson, London (1956 edition), Book 11, chap. 37-76, pp. 131-51.

28 Op. cit., Book IV, chap. 190, p. 362 [(emphasis added)].

29 Quoted by Frank Snowden Jr., in *Black in Antiquity: Ethiopians in the Greco-Roman Experience*, Cambridge (Mass.), 1970, p. 146.

30 *Works*, translated by C. H. Oldfather, London, 1955, Book 3, chap. 8, vol. II, pp. 103-5.

31 For full details, see Frank Snowden, op. cit., chap. VI.

32 Hannibal employed Negro soldiers in his army; the use of elephants in war was discovered by Africans at Meroë. The Romans were also involved with African peoples south of Egypt militarily and in diplomatic relations from the time of Augustus until late in the Empire.

33 See Mircae Elidae, *The Sacred and the Profane*, translated by Willard Trask, New York 1957, pp. 222-3; *Nuer Religions*, Oxford, 1956; *Bantu Philosophy*, Paris, 1959.

34 Frank Snowden, op. cit., chap. 3.

35 "Civilized man looks at Primitive Africa" in Ashley Montagu (editor), *The concept of the Primitive*, New York 1968, p. 178.

36 Hugh Trevor-Roper, *The Rise of Christian Europe*, London, 1964, pp. 9, 11.

37 *Politics* (translated by Benjamin Jowett) in *The Works of Aristotle Translated into English*, Oxford, 1921, Book I, ch. 5.

38 Catherine George, op. cit., p. 176.

39 Lewis Hanke, *Aristotle and the American Indian: A Study in Race Prejudice in the Modern World*, Bloomington, London, 1959.

40 N. Burkitt and N. W. G. Mackintosh, "Aborigines" in *Australia Encyclopedia*, 1958, pp. 2-3.

41 *The Rise of Christian Europe*, London, 1964, pp. 9, 11.

42 *The Scope of Anthropology*, translated by S. H. Paul and R. A. Paul, London, 1967, pp. 52-3.

43 The word "anthropologist" first appeared in Aristotle's *Nicomachean Ethics*, meaning one who tells anecdotes about men, a gossip.

44 Pagan derives from the Latin *paganus* meaning villager, [whereas] *pagus* is country. It later came to mean one who is not a Christian. Jesus Christ is the Greek form of Joshua the Messiah.

45 The killing of Jesus Christ is usually blamed on the Jews. Dimont has suggested that the story of the trial and killing were written not for the Jews but for the "pagan" world: the Thesalonieans, Philistians and Ephesians. Neither St. Paul nor the authors of the gospels would want to antagonize those they were seeking to convert, nor to anger the Roman rulers whom they had to mollify, especially since they could be thrown to the lions or crucified head down for such offences. For his rebuttal see *Jews, God and History*, New York, 1962, pp. 138-40.

46 Chap. 13.

47 In CE 165 Justin was executed by the order of the Governor Rusticus. During the trial the Governor told the prisoner "First of all obey the 'Roman' gods and make submission to the Princes." Justin replied, "To obey the commands of our Savior Jesus Christ is not worthy of blame or condemnation."

48 For the full story, see *The Essential Eusebius, the Story of the First Centuries of the Christian Church*, selected and translated by Colm Luibhcid, New York, 1966.

49 Max I. Dimont, *Jews, God and History*, p. 144.

## NOTES

[50] His work is entirely lost, but fortunately extensive excerpts are included in the reply by the Church Father Origen 246-248 CE. "Objections to the Idea of God coming down to earth," "Slanders against the Virgin," "On the Resurrection," "Miracles and Sorcery," "Christianity for fools only" and "Christian Propaganda" are found in *A New Etisebius: Documents Illustrative of the History of the Church, 337 CE,* edited by J. Stephenson, London, 1957, pp. 136-43. See also, *The True Word of Celsus, 177-180 CE,* from the translation of Jenry Charderic in *Origen: Contra Celcum,* Cambridge, 1953.

[51] J. B. Danquah, *The Akan Doctrine of God,* London, 2nd edition, 1968, p. 38; K. A. Busia, *Africa in Search of Democracy,* London, 1967, p. 4; E. Bojali Idowu, *Olodumare: God in Yoruba Belief,* London, 1963, p. 44.

[52] See F. L. Cross, *The Early Christian Fathers,* London, 1960, pp. 150-51.

[53] *The Marriage Customs of the Lango (Tribe) Uganda in relation to Canon Law,* Rome 1957, p. 55. The "civilized" Herodotus was amused at the "barbarians" who were shocked at nudity. He wrote, "For among the Lydians, and indeed among the barbarians generally, it is reckoned a deep disgrace, even to a man to be seen naked." For Herodotus a calm acceptance of nudity no less than an appreciation of beauty of form, was a sign of a civilized man. See *The History,* Book 1, chap. 10. Compare this with the attitude of the early Christian Fathers, who, emphasizing the teachings of St. Paul on celibacy attacked the habit of bathing on the ground that everything that made the body more attractive tended towards sin. St. Abraham the hermit who lived for fifty years after his conversion, rigidly refused to wash either his face or feet, and St. Amnion never saw himself naked. See Havelock Ellis, *Studies in the Psychology of Sex,* vol. IV, p. 13.

[54] *African Religions and Philosophy,* London and New York, 1969, p. 142.

[55] Marcus Manicus Felix, a distinguished African lawyer who lived in Rome during the third century, wrote his Apology in the form of a dialogue between a Christian called Octavius and a pagan by the name of Caelcilius. See "From Octavius" in *A new Eusibius,* p. 248.

[56] *Facing Mount Kenya,* London, 2nd ed., 1953, pp. 133-4. Jomo Kenyatta, now President of the Republic of Kenya led his people to *uhuru* ["freedom"] through one of Africa's bloodiest struggles. J. B. Danquah was known as the doyen of West African nationalism. He died while in detention in Ghana. K. A. Busia is now President of the Republic of Ghana. He was leader of the opposition during the Nkrumah regime. William Abraham was one of President Nkrumah's closest advisers.

[57] Solomon Katz, *The Decline and Fall of Rome and the Rise of Medieval Europe,* New York, 1967, p. 68.

[58] Quoted in Richard Bernheimer, *Wild Men in the Middle Ages,* Cambridge, 1952, p. 5. This authoritative work is the main source of my information.

[59] Ibid., p. 2.

[60] Lewis Hank, *Aristotle and the American Indians,* Bloomington and London, 1970, p. 3.

[61] See Alan Moorehead, *The White Nile,* London, 1960, p. 14, "By now that impenetrable blank space in the centre of the continent was filled in imagination with a thousand monstrosities, dwarf men and cannibals with tails, animals as strange as the fabulous griffin and the salamander..."

[62] See R. Palme Dutt, *The Crisis of Britain and the British Empire,* London, 1957, pp. 71-2.

[63] Roy Harvey Pearce, *Savagism and Civilization: A study in the Indian and the American mind,* Baltimore, 1967, p. 5.

[64] Catherine George, "Civilized Europe looks at Primitive Africa 1400-1800, a study in ethnocentricism," in *The idea of the Primitive,* ed. Ashley Montague, New York and London, 1968, pp. 186-7.

[65] Ibid., p. 139.

## NOTES

66 Raphael Pettazzoni, "The Formation of Monotheism," in *Reader in Comparative Religion*, eds. William A. Lessa and Evon Z. Vogt, New York, 1958, p. 40.

67 London, 1962, pp. 1-2 [(emphasis added)].

68 Quoted in Bertrand Russell, *A History of Western Philosophical Thought*, London, 1946, p. 363.

69 "Social Anthropology: Past and Present," in his *Essays in Social Anthropology*, London, 1962; *Theories of Primitive Religion*, Oxford, 1965, p. 18. See also Daryll Forde, "Tropical African Studies," *Africa*, vol. 35, no. 1, January 1965.

70 "The Structure of Unilineal Descent," *American Anthropologist*, vol. 53, no. I, pp. 17-18.

71 E. P. Dozier has made a strong plea for relinquishing such terms in favor of less loaded words. See his "The Concept of the 'Primitive' and 'Nature' in Anthropology" in *Year Book of Anthropology*, 1955.

72 "The Cultural Contributions and the prospects of Africa" in *Presence Africaine*, 1956, pp. 347-74.

73 *Negritude et Humanisme*, Paris, 1964, p. 24; see also *On Socialism*, London, 1964, p. 74.

74 *African Religions and Philosophy*, London and New York, 1969; *Concepts of God in Africa*, London and New York, 1970.

75 Evans-Pritchard, *Essays*, p. 35; *Concepts of God in Africa*, p. xiii.

76 *Theories of Primitive Religion*, p. 15.

77 London, 1928, p. 86.

78 *Civilization and its Discontents*, London, 1930, p. 23.

79 T. B. Bottomore, ed., *Karl Marx: Early Writings*, London, 1963, p. 167.

80 "Letter to Alexei Maximovich" in Rene Fulop-Miller, *Lenin and Gandhi*, London and New York, 1927, p. 152.

81 *The Golden Bough*, 1919, pp. 422-3.

82 *Essays*, pp. 40-41.

83 *Divinity and Experience*, p. 29.

84 *Documents of the Vatican II*, p. 586-97.

85 Later Pope Paul VI, "The Church," in *Masterpieces of Catholic Literature*, edited by Frank N. Magill, New York and London, 1965, p. 1119.

86 See Mircae Eliade, *The Sacred and the Profane: The nature of Religion*, translated by William R. Trask, New York, 1957, pp. 226-7.

87 See T. A. Beetham, *Christianity and the New Africa*, London, 1967, p. 7; A. F. C. Ryder, "Portuguese and Dutch in West Africa before 1800," in J. F, Ade Ajayi and Espie, eds., *A thousand years of West African History*, London, 1965, pp. 212-31.

88 Beetham, op. cit., pp. 8-9.

89 F. B. Welbourn, *East African Christian*, London, 1965, p. 64; J. F. A. Ajayi, *Christian Missions in Nigeria 1841-1871*, London, 1965, p. 14.

90 Quoted in A. F. C. Ryder, "Missionary activity in the kingdom of Warri to the early 19th century," *Journal of the Historical Society of Nigeria*, vol. 2, no. 1, 1960.

91 See C. J. Wilson, *Uganda in the days of Bishop Tucker*, London, 1955, p. 8.

92 First published in 1857, reprinted 1969, New York, pp. 68-9.

93 *Africa and Christianity*, Oxford, 1939, p. 94.

94 M. A. C. Warren, General Introduction to the Christian Presence Series. See John V. Tylor, *The Primal Vision: Christian Presence amid African Religion*, London, 1963, p. 10.

95 Op. cit.; see also Owen C. Thomas, *Attitudes towards other religions*, New York, 1968.

## NOTES

[96] *Christianity and the new Africa*, p. 22.

[97] "Dialogue with animism," in Jan Kerkhofs, ed., *Modem Mission Dialogue*, New York and London, 1968, p. 46.

[98] See *Bantu Philosophy*, 1959, chap. 2.

[99] *Nuer Religion*, Oxford, 1965, p. 116. See also J. P. Crazzolara, *A Study of the Acoli Language*, London, 1950, p. 240.

[100] See "Christians charged with atheism, at the instigation of demons" (Justin, Apology, I, 5-6) in *A New Eusebius, Documents illustrative of the history of the church, CE 337,* edited by J. Stephenson, London, 1957, pp. 62-3.

[101] "On the meaning of contemporary atheism," *Review of Politics*, vol. 11, July 1949, p. 267.

[102] C. A. Wright, "The supreme being among the Acholi of Uganda—another viewpoint," *Uganda Journal*, vol. 7, no. 3, January 1940.

[103] W. C. Willoughby, *The Soul of the Bantu*, London, 1910, p. xx.

[104] *Lectures on the origin of religion*, London, 1910, p. 49.

[105] *African Ideas of God*, London, 1950; *African traditional religions*, London, 1963, p. 43; *The Primal Vision*, London, 1963, p. 83.

[106] John Mbiti, *Concepts of God in Africa*, London and New York, 1970, p. xv.

[107] "Christianity and the other great religions," in *Soundings: Essays in Christian Understanding*, Cambridge, 1966, p. iii.

[108] African scholars studying African religions have not broken any new ground either in the methods of carrying out research or in their interpretations of the data collected. The most active ones today are Christian priests, and they appear to rely a great deal on published sources. These works must be subjected to thorough and critical analysis before we can use them as authorities.

[109] See J. P. Crazzolara, *Uganda Journal*, vol. 7, p. 135.

[110] See *The Origin of Life and Death: African Creation Myths*, ed. Ulli Beier, London, 1966, p. 57; see also John Mbiti, *Poems of Nature and Faith*, Nairobi, 1969, pp. 56-9, where the same story is rendered very beautifully into a poem in English entitled, "Man's loss of immortality."

[111] See K. A. Busia, *Africa in Search of Democracy*, London, 1967, p. 4.

[112] Quoted in Godfrey Lienhardt, *Man, Culture and Society*, p. 313.

[113] *The Primal Vision*, p. 89.

[114] "The idea of God among South African Bantu Tribes" in *African Ideals of God*, p. 102.

[115] See Evans-Pritchard, "Religion and the anthropologists," in his *Essays in Social anthropology*, London, 1964, pp. 29-45.

[116] Op. cit., in *Man, Culture and Society*, p. 320

[117] *Social Anthropology*, London, 1964, p. 84.

[118] *Essays in Social Anthropology*, p. 35.

[119] See Evans-Pritchard, *Theories of Primitive Religion*, Oxford, 1965, p. 91. See also, Max Muller, *Lectures on the Origin of Religion*, pp. 93-4. Garry W. Trompf wrote, "Conservative Oxford was not the place in which enthusiasts for non-Christian religious ideas could sparkle. If there were enthusiasts, the overpowering dominance of the High Church party tended to subdue them or forced them to couch their ideas in more apologetic, sometimes reactive language, rather than to present learned or popular treatises ready for immediate cash value on the intellectual market." See his, "Fredrick Max Muller: Some preliminary chips from his German Workshop," *The Journal of Religious History*, vol. 5, no. 3, June 1969, p. 214.

[120] *Loka* means the other side of the Victoria Nile, that is, Bunyoro.

[121] John A. T. Robinson, *Honest to God*, London, 1963, pp. 125-6.

122 These feasts are fast dying out as a result of the new political situation.
123 Gunter Wagner in *African Worlds*, ed. Daryll Forde, Oxford, 1954, pp. 28-30.
124 M. G. Whisson, *Change and Challenge*, Nairobi, 1964, p. 3.
125 Op. cit., pp. 28-30.
126 From *lak*, [meaning] "to spread out."
127 *Political System of the Anuak*, London, 1940, p. 75.
128 "The Shilluk of the Upper Nile," *African Worlds*, pp. 154.
129 *Politics*, Book 1, chap. 2.
130 "Luo tribes and clans," *Rhodes Livingstone Journal*, no. 7, 1949, pp. 24-40.
131 Bethwell Alan Ogot, *History of the Southern Luo*, Nairobi, East African Publishing House, 1965, p. 186.
132 *Nuer Religion*, pp. 106.
133 In the Old Testament, God is referred to in three ways: as "Elohim," "God," as "JHVR," "Lord" and as "Elohim JHVR," "Lord God." The orthodox Jew never pronounces the name "MYR." No one knows how the name was pronounced originally, since its utterance was already forbidden by the second century BCE.
134 *Jeremiah*, chap. XLIV, 14-17.
135 *I Maccabeas*, chap. 1, 60-63.
136 See Eugen Kullmann, "Alexandrian Philosophy," in *A History of Philosophical System*, ed. Vergilius Fern, New York, 1950, pp. 133-4.
137 William Ralph Inge, "The Theology of the Fourth Gospel," in *Cambridge Biblical Essays*, London, 1909, p. 257.
138 St. John's Gospel, chap. 1, 1-3, 14.
139 *Theories of Primitive Religion*, p. 14.
140 Jesus Christ disappears completely from the Gospel story at the age of about 12. The next we hear of him he is thirty. He appears briefly and dramatically before he is killed. Some scholars now suggest that during this long period he might have been among the party of Essenes whose headquarters was discovered recently near Jerusalem.
141 Vergilius Fern, "Early Christian Philosophy," in *A History of Philosophical System*, p. 144.
142 *Future of Belief*, p. 138.
143 *Oxford Dictionary of the Christian Church*, 1957, p. 940.
144 W. E. Abraham, *The Mind of Africa*, 1962, p. 55.
145 John Mbiti, *African Religions and Philosophy*, p. 29.
146 For a fuller discussion, see Bertrand Russell, *History of Philosophy*, London, 1946, pp. 67-71.
147 *The Akan Doctrine of God*, London, 1944, pp. 28, 30.
148 See *African Religions and Philosophy*, p. 30.
149 *Ancient Greece in African Political Thought*, Nairobi, 1967, p. 12.
150 One is reminded of a report by the missionaries A. L. Kitching and A. B. Lloyd when they were forced to leave Acoliland because of the withdrawal of the government from that area, "The people learning that we were off, hung round us like vultures, waiting for the little bit of rubbish we might throw aside while packing our odds and ends." C.M.S. Report 1905-1906, pp. 73-4.
151 *Towards the Conversion of England*, 1945, ch. 1.
152 *The Future of Belief*, London, 1967.
153 M. A. C. Warren, "Introduction," in John Taylor, *The Primal Vision*, London, 1963, p. 7.

## NOTES

[154] Quoted in John F. Kelly, "Aeterni Patris," in *Masterpieces of Catholic Literature*, New York and London, 1965, p. 694.

[155] Ibid.

[156] *The Revolution in Philosophy*, London, 1963, p. 3.

[157] See D. F. Pears, "Logical Atomism, Russell and Wittgenstein," in *The Revolution in Philosophy*, pp. 41-55

[158] J. Ayer, *Language Truth and Logic*, Oxford, 1946.

[159] *The Problems of Philosophy*, London, 1963, p. 141.

[160] Quoted in A. J. Ayer, *Philosophical Essays*, London, 1965, p. 231.

[161] *The Philosopher and Theology*, 1960; *The Christian Philosophy of St. Thomas Aquinas*, 1959; *Being and Some Philosophers*, 1949.

[162] See also his *Man and the State*, 1951, and *Moral Philosophy*, 1960.

[163] Op. cit., p. 42.

[164] *Prospects for Metaphysics*, ed. I. T. Ramsay, London, 1961, p. 80.

[165] "Beginning it all over again," in *Soundings: Essays in Christian Understanding*, Cambridge, 1966, pp. 17-18.

[166] See John A. T. Robinson and David L. Edwards, *The Honest to God Debate*, London, 1963; John A. T. Robinson, *The New Reformation?*, London, 1965; Daniel Jenkins, *Beyond Religion*, London, 1962; Gabriel Vahanian, *The Death of God*, New York, 1961; and *Wait Without idols*, New York, 1964.

[167] See his *Jesus, Kerygma and Myth: Primitive Christianity and in its Contemporary setting*, and *Theology of the New Testament*, 1-2.

[168] *Letters and Papers from Prison*.

[169] *The Shaking of the Foundation*, 1949; *Ultimate Concern*, 1965.

[170] *Church Dogmatics*, 4 vols.

[171] Op. cit., p. 42.

[172] Quoted in Godfrey Lienhardt, "Religion," in *Man, Culture and Society*, ed. Harry L. Shapiron, New York, 1960, p. 310.

[173] Op. cit., pp. 19-20.

[174] *African Religions and Philosophy*, London and New York, 1969, pp. 3-4.

[175] Op. cit., p. 2.

[176] Democritus, Epicurus and Lucertius (d. 55 BCE) were secularists.

[177] See his "Christian Faith and the growing power of Secularism," in *Religion and Culture: Essays in Honor of Paul Tillich*, ed. Walter Leibrecht, New York, 1959, p. 187.

[178] *Five stages of Greek religion*, p. 67

[179] St. Augustine was born in 354 CE at Tagast near the present town of Bone in Algeria. His father was a pagan and his mother a Christian. He was not baptized as a child nor did he become a Christian in his youth. For nine years as a student and then lecturer at Carthage he believed in Manichaeism—a religion which claimed that there were two gods: the god of good and the god of evil. Augustine was about thirty years old when he became converted to Christianity and was baptized in Rome by Ambrose. In his Confessions, written soon after becoming bishop of Hippo, he tells how he was tormented by sin, especially those committed when he was younger. The theft of a pear in his childhood troubled him deeply.

[180] *St. Mark*, XVI, 15.

[181] *Der Atheismus and siene Geschichte*, Stuttgart and Berlin, 1920-23.

182 Solon T. Kimball, "Introduction," in Arnold van Gennep, *Rites of Passage*, translated by Monika B. Vizedom and Gabrjelle L. Caffee, Chicago, 1960, p. xvii; Evans-Pritchard, *Theories of Primitive Religion*, pp. 112-13.

183 M. Fortes, *Social Anthropology at Cambridge since 1900*, Cambridge, 1953, p. 4. Lucy Mair wrote, "Researches with a practical bearing were also undertaken by the research institutes sponsored by the Colonial Office. Such institutes existed in East, West and Central Africa, in the West Indies and in Malaya. Makerere Institute of Social Studies carried out researches in the social consequences of the immigration of labor, the reasons for the ineffectiveness of African village headmen as agents of government policy, and the changing position of African chiefs. It also carried out a five-year study of urbanization." See her "Applied Anthropology," in *Encyclopedia of Social Sciences*.

184 See, *Africa*, vol. XXXV, no. 1, January 1965, pp. 38-9.

185 *African Religions and Philosophy*, pp. 1-2.

186 *Primal Vision*, p. 90.

187 Thomas Aquinas, *Collected Works*, ed. M. C. D'Arcy, London, 1939, p. 97.

188 *Concepts of God in Africa*, pp. xiv-xv.

189 *On African Socialism*, New York, 1964, p. 26.

190 "Ujamaa—the basis of African Socialism," in *African Socialism*, ed. William Friedland and Carl Rosberg Jr., Stanford, 1964, pp. 238-47.

191 *Philosophical Dictionary*, see in *Portable Voltaire*, ed. Ben Ray Redman, New York, 1969, p. 54.

192 *Men Without God?* p. 29.

193 Uganda Government, *Report of the Commission on Marriage, Divorce and the Status of Women* (also known as the Kalema Report), 1965; Republic of Kenya, *Report of the Commission on the Law of Marriage and Divorce*, Nairobi, 1968; and *Report of the Commission on the Law of Succession*, Nairobi, 1968; See also Tanner, "The codification of customary Law in Tanzania," *East African Law Journal*, vol. 2, 1966.

194 "Law Reform in Kenya," *East African Law Journal*, vol. 5, 1969, p. 54.

195 *Commission... Law of Succession* 11-13, p. 3.

196 *Corinth*, chap. 5, 1-5, see also *Ephesians*, chap. 5, 3-6. I *Timothy*, chap. 5, 9-12, we read that young widows must not be admitted into the church, "for when they wax wanton against Christ, they will many." In 2 *Timothy*, chap. 22, Christians are advised to "Flee also youthful lusts." Titus, chap. 2, 5-6, young men and women told to be chaste. *Hebrew*, chap. 13, 4, whoremongers and adulterers are threatened with God's judgment.

197 *Corinth*, chap. 7, 1-2; 8-9.

198 *Luke*, chap. 7, 45-50.

199 *John*, chap. 8, 3-11.

200 *Luke*, chap. 10, 38-42.

201 *John*, chap. 2, 1-10.

202 *Random House Dictionary of the English Language*, New York, 1967, p. 558.

203 *Primal Vision*, p. 110. Priestly celibacy has been defended in the following terms, "The chastity which is practiced on behalf of the heavenly Kingdom" (Mt. 19:12), and which the religious profess, deserves to be esteemed as a surpassing gift of grace. "For it liberates the human heart in a unique way (cf. 1 Cor. 7-32-33) and causes it to burn with greater love for God and all mankind". See, *Documents of Vatican II*, p. 474.

204 *The Challenge of Nationhood*, London, p. 76; See also I. R. Sinai, *The Challenge of Modernization*, London, 1964, chap. 4.

# INDEX

*abila* (ancestral shrine) 35, 38
Aborigines 3, 5, 10, 16, 21, 62 n. 40
Aborigines Protection Society 3
*Abosomsom* xxviii, xxxi
Abraham, W. 21, 33, 41-42, 63 no. 56, 66 n. 144
Acholi xxxvii, 6, 46-47, 62 n. 25, 65 n. 102
African deities xxvii, 4, 9, 12, 19-23, 29, 32-33, 39, 42-43, 46, 49-50, 51, 53
African ethics 51
African history 10, 64 n. 87
African institutions 3, 6, 17, 20, 55
African languages xvi, xviii, xx-xxi, 29, 46
African leaders 52-53, 55-56
African philosophy xi-xxi, xxxvi, 51
African religion(s) xiv, xxi-xxii, xxvi-xxviii, xxx, 1, 9, 13, 19-23, 25-26, 30-32, 39, 42, 49-53, 56, 63 n. 54, 65 n. 108
*African Religions and Philosophy*. See also John Mbiti xxvii
*African Religions in Western Scholarship*. See also Okot p'Bitek xxxvi
African scholars 4, 12-13, 20-21, 30, 32-33, 43
African socialism 52-53
African societies xxvi, 5, 10, 16-17, 23, 41, 46, 49, 55
African states 11
African thought systems xiii-xxii, xxvi, xxxv-xxxvii, 56
*African Traditional Religion: A Definition*. See also Bolaji Idowu xxxi, xxxv
African university xiii, 3
Agnostics 22
Akan cosmology/religion xxiii, xxxi, xxxiii
Akan language xvii, xxi, xxiii, xxx-xxxv
Akan people xv, xviii, xx-xxxvii
Akwapim (an Akan people) xxxii
Ancient Egypt 9-10, 12, 21, 39
Ancient Nubia 9
Animism xxv, 19-20, 26-27, 50
Anti-Semitism 13
*Anyamesom* xxviii
Aristotle 10, 38, 62 n. 37, 63 n. 60,
Ashanti (Asante) people 5, 33

Asia Minor (western Asia) 13
Atheists 22, 29, 52
Australia 2-3, 5, 10, 16, 21, 62 n. 40
Bantu people xviii, 36, 61 n. 23
Bantu philosophy xvii-xviii, xix, xxi, 26
Bantu religion 10, 52, 65 n. 114
Belief in God xxii, xxviii, xxix-xxx, 26, 30
Berlin conference (ca. 1884-85) 25
British Colonization Society 3
British empire 2
Busia, Kofi A. xxxiii, 12, 19, 21, 33, 42
Catholic church 25, 43-44
Catholic priests xxxvii, 29-30
Chiefdom xxxvii, 6, 35-38, 52-53
China xvi, 2
Christian church 13, 25-26, 41, 43, 62 n. 48
Christian faith. See also Christianity 2, 22, 25, 29, 32, 43-45, 49, 52, 56
Christian God xxx, 4, 19, 21-23, 29, 31-33, 37, 39, 42-43, 46, 49-52
Christian mission to Africa xxxvii, 25
Christian morality 12, 25, 43, 54
Christian philosophy 43
Christian prejudices 51
Christian teaching 29
Christianity. See also Christian faith xiv-xv, xxii, xxviii, xxx-xxxi, xxxvi, 11-13, 20-22, 26, 29, 30, 32, 35, 40, 42, 45, 49, 53-54
Colonial administration 3, 6
Colonial system/enterprise 1, 3, 7, 10, 49-50
Colonialism xi, xix, xxi, 1
Colonized Africans xiii, xiv, xxxi, 1
Communal philosophy xix-xx, xxxii, xxxv
Communism 55
Comte, Auguste 20
Concept of God xxii, xxx-xxxi, xxxvi, 31, 41, 45
Congo (Kinshasa) 6, 25, 42
Culture x-xxii, xxviii, xxxvi, 3, 6, 9, 12-3, 19-22, 26, 36, 49
Danquah, J. B. xxv, xxxv, 12, 19, 21, 33, 42
Dawson, Christopher 2
Decolonization xi, xiv-xxi, xxxvi-xxxvii

# INDEX

Democracy 10
Detribalization 7
Diodorus 9, 11
Diop, Cheikh Anta 21
Egyptian civilization 12, 21
English Parliament 2
Ethiopia 6, 9, 25
Ethiopian Orthodox Church 25
Ethnocentricism 9, 63 n. 64
Europe x, xvi, 1, 13, 25, 40, 43, 45, 49
European barbarians 21
European settlers 2
Evangelical revival in Europe 25
Evans-Pritchard 6, 9, 19, 22-23, 29, 32, 37-38, 41, 50-52
Exploitation 1-2, 7
Fetishism 20, 27, 50
Fortes, Meyer 5, 21, 50
Freud, Sigmund 22, 43
*gemo* (dwarfs that travel by night) 38
Ghana xiii, xv, xvii, xix, 63 n. 56
Gilbert, Sir Henry 1
Gilgamesh (Babylonian epic) 15
Greek deities/mythology 9
Greenberg, Joseph H. 5
Gyekye, Kwame xxv, xxviii
Hawkins, John 1
Hellenic/Hellenization 19, 21, 39-45, 50-51
Herodotus 9, 11
High God xxxvi, xxxvii, 27, 29, 31, 35, 52
Homer 9, 49
Hume, David xii, xxix, 19-20
Ibo (Igbo) 6
Idowu, Bolaji xxxi, 12, 21, 33, 42
*Imana* xxxvi
Imperialism 10, 25-26, 55
Intellectual colonization xiv
Islam xiv, 39
Ivory Coast xvii
Jerusalem 39-40
Jesuits 25
Jewish Christianity 40
Jews 11-13, 31, 39-40
*Jok* (pl. *jogi*) vii, xxxvii, 29, 35-38
Judaism 32, 39-40, 56
*Juok* 37

Kagame, Alexis xviii
Kenya 6, 36-38, 53-54
Kenyatta, Jomo 13, 19, 21, 33, 42
Khoisan 2, 16
Kikuyu (Gikuyu) 7
*Kwoth* (Nuer) 22, 36, 38
*Lawino* x
Levi-Strauss, Claude 11
Lienhardt, Godfrey 19, 22-23, 32, 37, 51
Logic xii, xiv-xvi, xxi, xxix, xxxi, xxxvi, 44
Luo people (Uganda) x, xxxvi-xxxvii, 6, 29, 36-39, 61 n. 23
Luo religion xxxvi, 36-41
Luoland 6
Marx, Karl (Marxism) 1, 22, 43, 52, 55
Mbiti, John 22, 43
Mboya, Tom 56
Messianism 40
Metaphysics xii, xviii, xxvii, 43-44
Middle Ages 2, 13, 15, 45
Mill, John Stuart xxxv
Minkus, Helaine xxxii-xxxiv
Missionaries xxx, xxxvi-xxxvii, 19-21, 25-26, 29-32, 37, 41-42, 50-51, 66 n. 150
Modern world xiv, xv-xvi, 7
Monotheism 20, 39
Muller, Max F. 29-33, 65 n. 119
Nation building 4, 53
Nationalists 13, 19
*Negritude* 21
Negro Emancipation Society 3
*Nhialic* (Dinka) 23, 36
Nicean Creed 13
Nigeria 6, 26
Nilotic peoples 6, 29, 36-37, 40
*Nirvana (*Buddhism) 30
noble savage. See also *wild man*. 15-17, 49
Nuer 22, 29, 36-38, 52
Nyame ("Akan Creator") xxii, xxix, xxx, xxxiv-xxxv
*Nyasaye* (pl. *Nyiseche*) 36-37
Nyerere, Julius 52
*obibi* (ogre) 15-16
*Oboade* (Akan) xxii-xxiii, xxxiii
Ocol vii, x
*Odomankoma* (Akan) xxv

# INDEX

*Olodumare: God in Yoruba Belief.* See also Bolaji Idowu xxxi
*Onyankopon* (Akan) xxii, xxx
Opoku, Kofi Asare xxxv
Oruka, Odera xx
p'Bitek, Okot xxxvi-xxxvii
Papal Bull 2
Parrinder, Geoffrey 19, 21-22, 30
Polytheism 19-20
Proverb(s) xix, 30-31
*Religion of the Central Luo.* See also Okot p'Bitek xxxvi
Rousseau, Jean Jacques 19-20
*ruoth* (cf. *rwot* among the Central Luo) 38
São Paulo de Luanda 25
Secularism 46
Self-assertion 15-16
Senghor, Leopold Sedar 19, 21, 42, 52
Slave trade 2, 16, 25
Slavery 2, 10
Smith, Edwin 19, 30-32
Social anthropology x, 1-3, 5, 50
*Song of Lawino.* See also Okot p'Bitek x, 61 n. 1
St. Augustine 12, 15, 29, 41, 49
Supreme Being/God xxii, xxiv, xxxii-xxxiii, 30, 33, 38, 41-42
Taylor, John 19, 30-31, 46, 52, 55
Tempels, (Father) Placide xvii-xix, 10, 19, 26, 52

*The Akan Doctrine of God.* See also J. B. Danquah xxv
The American Ethnological Society 2
The Americas 2, 5, 16
The Ethnological Society (London) 2-3
The Société Ethnologique (Paris) 2-3
Traditional religions xvi, xxvii-xxviii, xxx, 46, 51
Tribalism 6-7
Tswana 5-6
*Twediampon* (Akan) xxii
Uganda xxxvi, 6, 9, 10, 12, 15-16, 31, 36, 50, 52-53, 55
*uhuru* (freedom) 11, 50, 55-56, 63 n. 56
Unsikana (Xhosa convert) 31
*uThixo* 31-32
*West African Traditional Religion.* See also Kofi Asare Opoku xxxv
Western civilization 13, 15-16, 56
Western culture 20, 49
Western philosophy/thought xi, xiii, xvii, xxvi-xxvii, xxix, xxxiv
Western scholars 1, 3, 6-7, 10-11, 17, 19-20, 32-33
Western scholarship 3-5, 7, 9-10, 13, 19, 21, 49-50
*wild man.* See also *noble savage* 15-17
Williams, Eric 2
Xhosa 31-32
*yubbu abila* ("repairing the shrine") 38

www.ingramcontent.com/pod-product-compliance
Lightning Source LLC
Chambersburg PA
CBHW022019290426
44109CB00015B/1233